Praise for
SEAM

"Perfection breaks. *SEAM* bends—and wins. Mike Woodhouse delivers a bold framework that transforms flaws into fuel. Built for uncertainty, designed for action, *SEAM* is the playbook for leaders who thrive under pressure!"

RICH DIVINEY, retired Navy SEAL officer and author of *Masters of Uncertainty*

"Michael Woodhouse's book, *SEAM*, is spot on when it comes to the importance of both readiness and resiliency for today's leader, parent, or any organization. Instead of perfection, Michael suggests that the better quest is for a strategic yet flexible plan to adapt, or in some cases pivot, because of or in spite of change. Agility is key, as well as the belief that success is not flawlessness but rather the blend of 'great, good, and good enough.' *SEAM* provides the four components every leader needs to effectively navigate in a world that is continuously changing."

SUSAN HITE, CEO and innovator

"*SEAM* is a 'must-read' for all practitioners of planning, command and control, execution, and sustainment. Mike 'Woody' Woodhouse challenges the old conventions of 'seamlessness' and brings a superbly fresh perspective. Golden Dome, JADC2, and other practitioners of 'integration'—sit up and take notice!"

DAN KARBLER, lieutenant general, US Army, retired

"*SEAM* describes the fundamental flaws and impacts in prioritizing 'perfection' over iteration. Woody challenges the viewpoint that a monolithic uniform design is better than disparate pieces, organically constructed and integrated through interfaces. *SEAM* is a great, quick read for anyone dealing with what appears to be insurmountable projects. I highly recommend everyone read this book!"

DR. DEREK TOURNEAR, renowned leader and space professional

SEAM

THE ADAPTIVE STRATEGY FRAMEWORK FOR LEADERS

Mike "Woody" Woodhouse

amplify

www.amplifypublishing.com

SEAM: *The Adaptive Strategy Framework for Leaders*

©2025 Michael "Woody" Woodhouse. All Rights Reserved. No part of this publication may be reproduced, stored in a retrieval system or transmitted in any form by any means electronic, mechanical, or photocopying, recording or otherwise without the permission of the author.

The advice and strategies found within may not be suitable for every situation. This work is sold with the understanding that neither the author nor the publisher is held responsible for the results accrued from the advice in this book.

Although the author and publisher have made every effort to ensure that the information in this book was correct at press time, the author and publisher do not assume and hereby disclaim any liability to any party for any loss, damage, or disruption caused by errors or omissions, whether such errors or omissions result from negligence, accident, or any other cause.

For more information, please contact:
Amplify Publishing, an imprint of Amplify Publishing Group
620 Herndon Parkway, Suite 220
Herndon, VA 20170
info@amplifypublishing.com

Library of Congress Control Number: 2025904370
CPSIA Code: PRV0725A
ISBN-13: 979-8-89138-475-0

Printed in the United States

To Stacey, Maddox, and Owen

You are my greatest teachers, showing me daily how to navigate life's seams with courage, compassion, and unwavering love.

Your resilience, growth, and partnership inspire every page of this book, reminding me that true leadership lies in adapting to challenges while holding fast to what matters most.

This is for you, my heart and my home, as we strategize, execute, assess, and modify—together.

CONTENTS

Author's Note	i
Foreword by Beth Roden	iii
Chapter 1: The Birth of SEAM—Finding Power in the Seams	1
Chapter 2: Rethinking Strategy—Finding Strength in the Seams	13
Chapter 3: Embracing Imperfection—Turning Flaws into Strengths	27
Chapter 4: Strategize—the Power of Partial Framing	37
Chapter 5: Execution—from Plan to Impact	45
Chapter 6: Assessment—Measuring Success	55
Chapter 7: Modification—Embracing the "Same Difference"	63
Chapter 8: Strategic Harmony—Aligning Goals, Methods, and Resources	69
Chapter 9: Navigating Risk in an Uncertain World	79
Chapter 10: Harnessing Technology for Strategic Advantage	91
Chapter 11: SEAM in Action: Case Studies and Real-World Insights	97
Chapter 12: Shaping the Future of Strategy with SEAM	105
About the Author	113

AUTHOR'S NOTE

This book was born from a deep belief that embracing imperfection leads to growth, innovation, and real progress. I realized I was uniquely qualified to write about strategy, not just because of my academic background but because of my two decades of experience navigating complex, ever-shifting environments, from military operations to the corporate world.

Truth be told, I was advised not to write a book. "Articles will get more eyes," they said. But the more someone steers me away from something, the more determined I become to do it. And here's the thing: Countless books and articles on strategy are out there. So why write another? This book is different; it's not just another method. It's a framework that offers tools, options, and perspectives that can be applied as needed. It's about setting realistic expectations, not lowering standards, and creating strategies that thrive on uncertainty.

And I've kept it short for a reason. One of the core philosophies I live by is that "better is the enemy of good enough." While I could have spent years fine-tuning every word, I chose to get this on paper while the ideas were fresh and relevant. There will be time for further exploration and refinement later if more writing follows, but this is the best representation of how to approach strategy in the twenty-first century.

Before we dive in, I want to take a moment to thank those who have always inspired me to stay true to myself while adapting my ideas to the beautiful complexity of life.

To my family, my grandparents, parents, wife, children, and extended family, thank you for supporting me through every step of this journey. Your unwavering encouragement has been my greatest strength.

Thank you to my teachers and professors, military leaders, and countless coworkers, whether superiors or subordinates, who shared in the grind and contributed their knowledge along the way. You've shaped the person I am today, and I am endlessly grateful for that.

Foreword

BY BETH RODEN

Leadership in today's world is vastly different from what it once was. We are no longer operating in environments where precision, structure, and predictability rule the day. As a twenty-year veteran of the US Army with two leadership masters, my brother Mike has seen this shift firsthand. As a Lieutenant Colonel, a father of two sons, one of whom has diverse abilities, Mike has faced challenges that many would shy away from, and yet for him, it's done the opposite. He has embraced these challenges and sees only opportunities. These experiences have shaped his perspective on leadership.

Like many of us, Mike has spent years trying to implement strategies with the hope of flawless execution, always pursuing perfection. The world told us that with enough structure and meticulous planning, everything could go as we envisioned. But the reality? It doesn't always work that way. It was during a flight back to Washington, DC, from a military conference—one filled with endless PowerPoint presentations, each touting its own method for achieving organizational excellence—that Mike had an epiphany. Amid the mechanical hum of the plane, he found inspiration in its structure: the joints between panels, the rivets on the walls, and the connections between the wings and fuselage. These weren't imperfections; they were essential features that allowed the plane to function, to adapt, and to move through the air with resilience. A plane moves fluidly in the sky because of its seams, not because it is seamless.

It was in that moment, in the quiet of flight, that Mike realized the core truth that had been missing from his approach as a leader, a parent, and even as a person. The pursuit of perfection, the relentless quest to execute flawlessly, was not only unrealistic—it was counterproductive. Instead, what truly mattered was the ability to embrace the seams, the flaws, and the imperfections that allow us to adapt and grow. From this revelation, SEAM was born. A simple but powerful acronym designed to help us view our work, leadership, and life through a new lens: Strategize, Execute, Assess, and Modify.

SEAM is more than just a framework; it's a mindset. It's a call to action for those of us trying to navigate the complexities of leadership in an increasingly fluid world. With SEAM, Mike offers clear, actionable tools to guide us as we move through the four essential stages of strategy execution—tools that are not just theoretical but grounded in the real experiences of a military leader and a father.

Having been a corporate leader for over thirty years and a mother of three grown daughters, I have personally seen how SEAM can change the way I lead a team. SEAM can help a team embrace the fluidity of today's world, recognizing that striving for perfection is not the path to success. In a world that changes faster than ever before, SEAM gives you a framework to adapt to challenges, embrace differences, and navigate obstacles with greater agility.

This book is a quick read, but it's packed with real-world wisdom. Whether you are a parent, a leader, or simply someone striving to improve, Mike's experiences in both the military and family life offer invaluable insights that will help you adapt your leadership style to the demands of today's world.

If you are looking to lead with more flexibility, more authenticity, and more success, then this book is for you. Happy reading. Happy leading.

BETH RODEN
Leader, master communicator, and mother

Chapter 1

THE BIRTH OF SEAM— FINDING POWER IN THE SEAMS

"IN THE MIDDLE OF DIFFICULTY LIES OPPORTUNITY."
— Albert Einstein

It was yet another long flight back to the nation's capital. Looking through the airplane window at thirty thousand feet, I had an epiphany that would transform my understanding of strategy and leadership. The metal rivets along the walls, the joints between panels, the connections between wings and fuselage . . . they weren't flaws in the aircraft's design, but essential features. Each seam allowed for thermal expansion and contraction, distributed stress loads, and enabled the flexibility necessary for flight. Without these carefully engineered connection points, the plane would be rigid and brittle, more likely to crack under pressure than adapt to changing conditions.

The timing of this revelation was almost poetic. Just hours earlier, I had sat through yet another military conference in Los Angeles, an event that exemplified everything wrong with our current approach to organizational strategy. The atmosphere was familiar to anyone who's spent time in these circles: military leaders, defense contractors, and tech professionals gathered in dimly lit conference rooms, their faces illuminated by the glow of endless PowerPoint presentations.

"The more original a discovery, the more obvious it seems afterwards." Arthur Koestler's words echoed in my mind as I considered how we'd been getting it wrong all along.

THE SEAMLESS ILLUSION

The three-day conference had been a parade of presenters, each armed with sophisticated diagrams and complex flowcharts, all promising the holy grail of organizational effectiveness: *seamless integration*. Every speaker seemed to have their own proprietary solution for eliminating friction points, achieving perfect synchronization, and delivering flawless results.

The word "seamless" dominated every conversation, appearing with almost comical frequency: "seamless communication between units," "seamless coordination of resources," "seamless transition from planning to execution," and the ever popular "seamless integration of capabilities." The term appeared so often it began to sound like white noise, yet its premise went unchallenged.

In the coffee breaks between sessions, I found myself

increasingly troubled by this obsession with seamlessness. Having spent nearly two decades in military service and several years as an entrepreneur and philanthropist, I'd witnessed countless operations, projects, and initiatives. Not one of them had ever been truly seamless. More importantly, I was beginning to realize that the most successful ones hadn't succeeded despite their seams. They'd succeeded because of them.

As our plane continued its journey east, my mind wandered to other examples where seams prove essential rather than detrimental. I thought about the Earth's tectonic plates, massive sections of the planet's crust that meet at seams we call fault lines. While these seams can create challenges through earthquakes and volcanic activity, they're also crucial to the planet's ability to release internal pressure and maintain its dynamic equilibrium.

The Akashi Kaikyō Bridge in Japan is a masterpiece of seam utilization. Spanning nearly two and a half miles across the Akashi Strait, this engineering marvel remains standing not because it's a single, rigid structure, but because it incorporates carefully designed expansion joints, deliberate seams that allow the bridge to expand, contract, and flex with changing temperatures and loads. These seams enable the bridge to survive everything from daily temperature fluctuations to powerful earthquakes.

In the digital realm, where the pursuit of seamless integration reaches near religious fervor, the most robust and resilient systems succeed not by eliminating connections but by managing them effectively. The internet itself functions because of protocols that handle the seams between different networks. Cloud computing works because of well-managed interfaces between services. The most successful software architectures embrace modularity, a principle built on the idea that well-defined seams between components create more robust and adaptable systems.

The human body itself offers perhaps the most compelling example of the importance of seams. Our joints, the seams of our skeletal system, aren't weaknesses in our physical structure but the very features that enable movement and adaptation. The boundaries between different types of tissue, the synapses between neurons, the membranes between cells—all these seams work together to create not just functionality but life itself.

You don't have to look hard to find evidence that seams are not flaws to be avoided but integral to the functionality of the complex systems that make up our world.

FROM PERSONAL CATALYST TO PROFESSIONAL PARALLELS

In 2020, a personal experience crystallized these emerging thoughts about seams and systems. My five-year-old son was diagnosed with autism, and suddenly, every assumption I had about control, predictability, and seamless execution was challenged in the most intimate way possible.

As a military officer, I'd been trained to value structure, order, and predictability. My professional life revolved around creating and executing precise plans, minimizing variables, and maintaining control. But autism doesn't follow anyone's playbook. My son's behavior, brilliant but often erratic, defied conventional parenting approaches that emphasized consistent routines and predictable responses.

Initially, this unpredictability felt like failure, both his and mine. Traditional parenting strategies, with their emphasis on clear cause-and-effect relationships, proved woefully inadequate. Every day brought new challenges, unexpected reactions, and moments when carefully laid plans crumbled in the face of reality.

But gradually, through hours of trial and error, consultation with specialists, and deep reflection, my wife, Stacey, and I developed what we now call "proactive reactiveness," which we'll explore in chapter 5. Instead of trying to eliminate uncertainty, we learned to anticipate and embrace it.

The revelation that managing the seams was the key to supporting our son began illuminating patterns in my professional experience too. From 2019–2022, during my time as a NATO missile defense and space planner, I encountered a situation that exemplified the importance of embracing seams rather than trying to eliminate them.

Our alliance faced a significant challenge: integrating

various missile defense systems from different member nations. Each country had its own hardware and software, developed to meet its specific needs and budgetary constraints. The initial instinct was to push for a unified—yes, "seamless"—system that would work the same way across all allied nations.

However, we quickly realized that this approach was impractical. The long lead times for acquisition and the resource constraints unique to each nation made it nearly impossible to achieve true technological interoperability in any reasonable time frame.

Instead, we shifted our focus to what I now recognize as a "seam-centric" approach. Rather than trying to force disparate systems into a single mold, we concentrated on integrating procedures through training and education. We developed joint exercises and simulations that allowed operators from different nations to work together effectively, even while using their native systems.

This approach acknowledged and embraced the seams between different national capabilities, increasing our overall resilience and flexibility. By focusing on helping humans work together more effectively rather than standardizing all our technologies, we created a more adaptive and robust defense network.

The success of this approach showed that effective integration doesn't always mean eliminating differences. Sometimes, it means learning to work at the intersections, leveraging the unique strengths that each component brings to the whole.

This experience reinforced my growing understanding that seams, whether in personal life, organizations, or international alliances are not weaknesses to be eliminated, but critical features that enable flexibility, adaptation, and ultimately, resilience in complex systems.

THE SEAM FRAMEWORK TAKES SHAPE

On that flight back home, I opened my laptop and began writing what would become a blog post titled "Reviving the Seam: Redefining Joint Military Integration." Posted in late 2023, the article challenged the military's long-standing pursuit of seamless integration between units and operations, arguing instead for the recognition and optimization of strategic seams.

The response was immediate and much bigger than I'd anticipated. Within days, my inbox was flooded with messages from military officers, business leaders, and organizational specialists across the globe. Many shared their own experiences with the limitations and failures of pursuing seamlessness. Some described costly projects that had failed precisely because they'd tried to eliminate natural and necessary points of connection and friction.

From that point on, the SEAM framework began to take

shape. Drawing on the military's fondness for acronyms, I developed a structure that embraced seams while remaining practical and actionable:

- **Strategize:** Develop plans that acknowledge and leverage connection points. Rather than trying to eliminate friction, we identify where it can serve us. This means mapping out not just the components of our strategy but the critical points where they interact. These connection points become opportunities for adaptation and innovation rather than problems to be solved.

- **Execute:** Implement strategies with attention to managing critical interfaces. This involves developing specific protocols for managing transitions, establishing clear communication channels across boundaries, and maintaining flexibility at key connection points. The focus shifts from eliminating seams to optimizing them.

- **Assess:** Continuously evaluate how seams are functioning. This isn't about finding flaws but understanding opportunities. Regular assessment helps identify which seams are working well and which need attention. This ongoing evaluation process focuses not just on individual components but on the effectiveness of their interactions.

- **Modify:** Adjust the approach based on real-world feedback. Modification isn't a sign of failure but a critical component of success. This involves having clear protocols for implementing changes, ensuring that adaptations at one seam don't create problems at others, and maintaining overall system stability while allowing for necessary adjustments.

The SEAM Framework

STRATEGIZE

Develop plans that acknowledge and leverage connection points.

EXECUTE

Implement strategies with attention to managing critical interfaces.

ASSESS

Continuously evaluate how seams are functioning.

MODIFY

Adjust approach based on real-world feedback.

When we touched down in Washington, DC, I felt clearer than I had in years. This SEAM idea wasn't just about military strategy or business operations. It applied to leadership, innovation, and even life itself. We shouldn't be trying to eliminate seams—we need to work with them. These connection points represent our advantage, not our weakness.

This new understanding began to fundamentally change how I approached both professional and personal challenges. In my business ventures, this approach transformed our marketing and operations strategies. Rather than pursuing a single, seamless marketing plan, we developed a strategy that tapped into the unique strengths of various channels. We used social media for brand building and community engagement, email marketing for targeted promotions, and content marketing for education and trust building. Each channel had its own rhythm and best practices, and we didn't try to force them into perfect alignment. Our inventory management system was designed with intentional seams between different product categories, allowing us to respond quickly to market trends without disrupting the entire system. Our market research combined traditional surveys with social media listening, sales data analysis, and direct customer feedback. The seams between these different data sources often provided the most valuable insights, highlighting discrepancies that led to new understandings of our market.

Even in personal relationships, I recognized that the seams between different aspects of life—work, family, personal growth—weren't problems to be solved but opportunities to be managed. For example, instead of forcing a rigid separation between work life and family time, I started looking for ways to blend them in a healthy way, bringing my kids to the office for special events or dedicating specific evenings to family game nights with no work interruptions. I realized that embracing the seams, those moments of transition and connection, brought more harmony and balance to my life. Acknowledging and respecting the unique needs and boundaries of each area allowed me to move between them with more intention and less friction.

I also began to see how the implications of this approach extend far beyond individual projects, organizations, or families. The large-scale challenges we face, from economic instability to global security, cannot be solved through seamless integration. They require us to understand and effectively manage the countless seams—the ones between nations, cultures, technologies, and ideologies—that define our wider world.

This seam-centric perspective offers a new lens through which to view leadership and problem-solving. It encourages us to embrace complexity rather than shy away from it, to see connections as opportunities rather than obstacles. The leaders and organizations that thrive today and tomorrow will be those that master the art of navigating these seams with skill, creativity, and foresight.

That flight marked the beginning of a new way of thinking about strategy and leadership. The next chapters will explore each component of the SEAM framework in detail, showing how this approach can transform how we think about and execute strategy in any context. We'll examine real-world applications across military operations, business ventures, and personal challenges, providing practical tools for implementing this approach in your own context.

Welcome to a new way of thinking. Let's navigate the seams together.

Chapter 2

RETHINKING STRATEGY— FINDING STRENGTH IN THE SEAMS

"IN THE MIDST OF CHAOS, THERE IS ALSO OPPORTUNITY."
— Sun Tzu, *The Art of War*

Have you ever watched a meticulously crafted plan unravel in real time? Like a house of cards meeting a sudden gust of wind, even the most carefully constructed strategies can collapse when they encounter reality. This vulnerability often stems not from poor planning but from our assumptions about what makes a strategy effective.

I witnessed this firsthand during a complex military operation in Southwest Asia. Our team had spent weeks developing what we thought was an airtight strategy for a time-sensitive, complex operation. Our plan accounted for every conceivable variable: readiness posture, personnel allocation, threat levels, and even weather patterns. However, within hours of implementation, we were forced to adapt rapidly. Human errors in asset counting, failures in status reporting, and the creeping effects of fatigue among our teams threw our plan into disarray. We had to make swift, on-the-fly adjustments to our carefully crafted strategy.

For decades, organizations have pursued strategies built on the premise of control, detailed plans designed to eliminate uncertainty and ensure predictable outcomes. Yet time and again, this approach proves inadequate in the face of real-world complexity. This chapter explores why traditional approaches fall short and introduces a new way of thinking about strategy that finds strength in the very elements we typically try to eliminate.

THE MYTH OF PERFECT CONTROL

Traditional strategic planning operates on several core assumptions that deserve scrutiny.

First is the belief that with enough analysis and preparation, we can anticipate and control all variables. This illusion of control has led countless organizations down expensive paths of overplanning and rigid execution. Consider the fate of Kodak, which developed the first digital camera in 1975 but clung to its traditional film strategy, unable to adapt when the market shifted dramatically toward digital photography. Their detailed plans and market dominance couldn't save them from disruption because they were optimized for a world that was rapidly disappearing.

I encountered this mindset repeatedly while overseeing military integration projects. Teams would spend months creating elaborate implementation plans, trying to account for every possible contingency. Yet inevitably, the most successful projects were those that maintained flexibility at key connection points, the seams where different systems, teams, and capabilities intersected.

Second is the assumption that stability is the natural state of business, and that disruption is an anomaly to be avoided. Yet history shows us that change is the only constant. The rise of Amazon didn't just disrupt retail; it transformed consumer expectations across all industries. Companies that treated this disruption as a temporary blip found themselves increasingly irrelevant.

THE SEAM APPROACH TO STRATEGY: TWO CASE STUDIES

The SEAM framework represents a fundamental shift in how we think about strategy, from trying to eliminate uncertainty and control every variable to embracing the dynamic nature of modern environments. I'll share two case studies that illustrate SEAM in action before diving into the details of the framework.

TURNING SETBACK INTO OPPORTUNITY WITH THE PATRIOT BROS. ASSOCIATION

In my early days as a designer, I encountered an unexpected seam that ultimately became the catalyst for a new opportunity. Initially, I had designed and marketed morale merchandise (stickers, patches, keychains, etc.) and apparel with the intention of voluntarily contributing it to an established, well-respected organization. My vision was clear: Create products that would boost morale and support our soldiers. And on paper, the organization I'd targeted seemed like a great candidate for this vision: They were well-known as the premier destination for these kinds of products, and their current inventory had become outdated. However, I soon discovered a significant disconnect.

The organization, despite its reputation, struggled to grasp the potential of my initiative. They hesitated to accept what was essentially a free resource that could inevitably benefit them. But rather than viewing this as a setback, I sensed an opportunity. The hesitation I encountered revealed a gap in the market, a seam between existing support structures and the evolving needs of our military community.

Instead of trying to force my vision into an existing framework, I decided to leverage this seam by establishing my own 501(c)(3) organization, The Patriot Bros. Association. The mission of the Patriot Bros. Association is to increase awareness and spread "esprit de corps" within Air Defense

Artillery via Air Defense–themed media and merchandise, with the ultimate goal of providing scholarship opportunities to deserving individuals in the Air Defense community.

The creation of Patriot Bros. allowed us to not just fill a gap, but create a new model for soldier support that was more agile, more responsive to current needs, and more aligned with contemporary marketing strategies. By recognizing and capitalizing on this seam, we created an organization that could effectively serve both the soldiers we aimed to support and the civilian population eager to contribute to their well-being.

At the time of authoring this book, the Patriot Bros. have awarded thirteen scholarships worth over $50,000 and donated countless merchandise as care packages to soldiers stationed and deployed worldwide.

TESLA'S MANUFACTURING EVOLUTION

Let's look at another real-world example of finding strength in seams: Tesla's approach to automobile manufacturing. Traditional auto manufacturers spent decades perfecting "seamless" production lines designed to minimize variation and maximize efficiency. Tesla, however, took a different tack.

Rather than trying to eliminate production seams, Tesla designed its manufacturing process to be highly adaptable. Their factory floors can be reconfigured quickly, and their software-first approach allows for rapid iterations in both product design and production methods. When COVID-19 disrupted global supply chains, this flexibility proved invaluable. While traditional manufacturers struggled with rigid processes, Tesla could adapt its production methods and components more readily.

The company's approach to battery production offers another illustrative example. Instead of trying to create a seamless battery manufacturing process, Tesla designed their battery packs with distinct modules. This approach, while creating more obvious seams in the production process, allows for easier maintenance, upgrades, and adaptation to new battery technologies as they emerge.

THE FOUR DIMENSIONS OF STRATEGIC SEAMS

In the rest of this chapter, I'll provide an overview of where the strategic seams exist in an organization and how leaders can begin to appreciate, manage, and tap the potential of those seams.

Understanding how to leverage seams first requires recognizing their four key dimensions: organizational, market, technological, and temporal.

1. Organizational Seams
These exist between different departments, teams, or

functions within an organization. Traditional thinking sees these as efficiency drags that should be minimized. However, these intersection points often drive innovation and adaptation. During my military career, I saw how the seams between intelligence, operations, and logistics units often generated the most innovative solutions to complex challenges. When these units maintained rigid boundaries, effectiveness suffered. But when they created flexible interfaces while maintaining their distinct specialties, the force as a whole became more capable.

2. Market Seams

These occur at the boundaries between different market segments or customer needs. Amazon Web Services (AWS) emerged from Amazon's recognition of a seam between traditional IT infrastructure and emerging cloud computing needs. By exploring this seam rather than avoiding it, they created an entirely new market category. I've seen similar dynamics in defense contracting, where the most successful companies are those that identify and leverage the seams between different military requirements, civilian applications, and emerging technological capabilities.

3. Technological Seams

These exist at the intersections of different technologies or capabilities. Google's success with Android came from recognizing and leveraging the seam between mobile phones and internet services, creating a platform that could evolve with both technologies. In missile defense systems, we learned to value the seams between different detection, tracking, and intercept technologies. Rather than trying to create a monolithic system, we developed flexible interfaces that allowed us to upgrade individual components without compromising the entire network (as you'll learn later in this chapter).

4. Temporal Seams

These occur during transitions between different states or phases of strategy. Netflix's transition from DVD rental to streaming exemplifies successful navigation of a temporal seam, maintaining business continuity while fundamentally transforming their service model.

The Four Dimensions of Strategic Seams

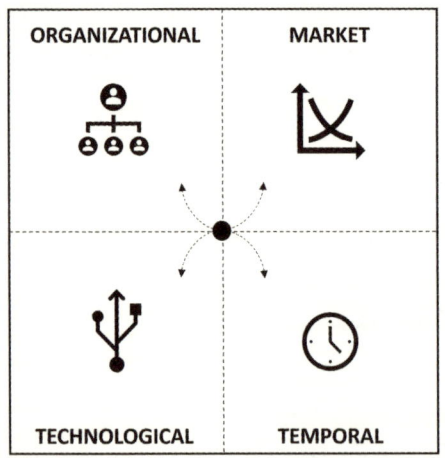

THE PRACTICE OF STRATEGIC SEAM MANAGEMENT

Managing strategic seams effectively requires a different mindset and toolset than traditional strategic planning. Organizations can develop this capability with a three-part framework of seam identification, analysis, and optimization. Here's how to go about it.

1. Seam Identification
Start by creating a comprehensive map of your organization's strategic landscape:

- **Interfaces**: Where do different departments, teams, and functions interact, such as handoffs between sales, marketing, and product development?
- **Capability gaps**: What connections exist between your current capabilities and future opportunities, including skills, expertise, and infrastructure requirements?
- **Customer journey**: Where do your customers' needs intersect with emerging technologies, and how can you enhance or disrupt the customer experience?
- **Ecosystem interactions**: What relationships exist between your organization and external stakeholders, including partners, competitors, and suppliers?

This process requires both systematic analysis and intuitive understanding of your organization and its ecosystem, combining data-driven insights with human judgment and expertise.

2. Seam Analysis
Next, evaluate the strategic potential of each seam:
- **Opportunities**: What possibilities exist at this intersection, such as new business models, products, or services?
- **Risks**: What challenges need to be managed, such as operational complexities, regulatory issues, or competitor activity?
- **Evolution**: How might this seam change over time, and what implications might this have for your organization's strategy and operations?

This analysis should be flexible and ongoing, recognizing that seams aren't static but require continuous attention and adjustment.

3. Seam Optimization
Then start to develop approaches to leverage the seams you've identified:
- **Flexible interfaces**: Build adaptable connections between different organizational units, enabling seamless communication and collaboration.
- **Adaptive processes**: Create processes that can respond to changing conditions, such as shifting

customer needs or emerging technologies.
- **Feedback mechanisms**: Establish monitoring systems to track seam health, identify potential issues, and facilitate continuous improvement. By optimizing your strategic seams, you can unlock new opportunities, mitigate risks, and drive long-term success.

My experience with missile defense systems is an example of seam management in practice. Modern air defense requires coordination between multiple radar systems, missile batteries, and command centers. Traditional thinking would try to eliminate the seams between these components through rigid integration protocols, but we found greater success by working with these seams. By creating flexible interfaces between systems, we could add new capabilities or swap out components with less disruption to the network, allowing us to integrate new threats and countermeasures without rebuilding the entire system.

One incident stands out. During a major exercise, we lost connectivity with a key radar system. In a rigidly integrated system, this would have crippled our defenses. However, because we had designed our interfaces to be flexible, other radars could quickly adjust their coverage patterns, maintaining effective defense while the failed system was repaired.

BUILDING SEAM-AWARE ORGANIZATIONS

Developing an organization that can effectively leverage seams requires several key elements.

First, there's establishing a **cultural readiness** for this shift. This means fostering openness to change and experimentation, encouraging cross-functional collaboration, and rewarding innovative solutions that bridge organizational divisions.

Next is allowing **structural flexibility**, designing (or redesigning) the organization to be able to reconfigure easily, creating clear but adaptable interfaces between units, and maintaining clear communication channels across seams.

Then there's facilitating appropriate **leadership capability**: developing leaders who can think systemically, be comfortable with ambiguity and change, and encourage balanced risk-taking.

Last but not least, **measuring success** of your seam management approach requires a different approach than traditional metrics allow. Consider measuring:

- Adaptation speed when conditions change
- Innovation emerging from organizational intersections
- Resilience during market disruptions
- Value created through cross-functional initiatives

For instance, in military operations, we created measures to evaluate not just individual unit performance but the effectiveness of inter-unit coordination and adaptation.

YOUR COMPETITIVE ADVANTAGE LIES IN THE SEAMS

As organizations face increasing complexity and rapid change, the ability to manage seams effectively becomes more crucial. Future success will depend not on eliminating these connection points but on leveraging them for competitive advantage.

The next chapter will look at the power of imperfection, before we explore how the SEAM framework's components—Strategize, Execute, Assess, and Modify—work together to create strategies that don't just survive complexity but thrive on it, helping build more-resilient organizations that can adapt and evolve in an increasingly uncertain world.

Chapter 3

EMBRACING IMPERFECTION—TURNING FLAWS INTO STRENGTHS

> "AS MACHINES BECOME MORE AND MORE EFFICIENT AND PERFECT, SO IT WILL BECOME CLEAR THAT IMPERFECTION IS THE GREATNESS OF MAN."
> —**Ernst Fischer,** *The Necessity of Art*

In both military and business circles, we chase perfection like a mirage in the desert—always visible on the horizon but perpetually out of reach. Strategic planning often falls prey to this obsession with flawlessness. We convince ourselves that with enough analysis, preparation, and control, we can create perfect plans that execute without deviation.

Throughout my career in defense systems, I observed a common pattern across large-scale technical projects. Teams would often become consumed by the quest for perfect integration, investing enormous resources into eliminating every conceivable vulnerability. This obsession with absolute reliability typically spawned increasingly complex solutions, adding layers of redundancy and fail-safes. Ironically, these elaborate measures often made systems more fragile and less effective when deployed in actual operational environments. What began as prudent risk management would evolve into counterproductive overengineering, undermining the very reliability we sought to achieve.

In reality, the most successful strategies often succeed not despite their imperfections but because of them. These "flaws" provide the flexibility and adaptability needed to navigate an unpredictable world. This chapter explores how embracing imperfection can transform our approach to strategy, leadership, and organizational success.

THE ILLUSION OF PERFECT PLANNING

Consider a recent experience from my defense industry work. During the planned deployment of new demonstration systems intended for training purposes, our carefully orchestrated timeline encountered significant supply chain disruptions. Traditional thinking would have viewed this as a major setback—a disruption to our perfect training schedule. Instead, it became a compelling example of how unexpected constraints can drive innovation.

The demonstration systems were delayed beyond their planned training window—a scenario we had contemplated but hoped to avoid. Rather than rigidly adhering to the original schedule, our teams pivoted. They developed and implemented a sophisticated virtual training environment while working with vendors to repurpose the delayed systems. What began as a scheduling "failure" became an unexpected advantage: The systems were ultimately delivered during the operational window, with enhanced capabilities and redundancy that exceeded our initial requirements. This adaptation not only maintained our readiness but improved our overall operational capacity beyond the original plan.

This pattern repeats across industries. When Apple launched the first iPhone, it lacked features that seemed essential at the time—copy and paste, third-party apps, even picture messaging. Yet these "imperfections" allowed Apple to focus on core functionality and user experience, while creating space for iterative improvements that would define the smartphone era. Or take SpaceX's approach to rocket development. Rather than pursuing perfect designs through endless simulation and testing, they embrace a rapid prototyping and testing cycle that accepts and learns from failures. As Elon Musk noted, "Failure is an option here. If things are not failing, you are not innovating enough."

THE PATRIOT: A CASE STUDY IN PROGRESSIVE IMPERFECTION

The Patriot missile system is one of the most sophisticated air and missile defense platforms in the world, yet its development illustrates a fundamental truth about complex systems: Perfection is neither achievable nor desirable. As a tactical control officer and test detachment commander, I witnessed firsthand how accepting and working with imperfections became the catalyst for major improvements.

When first deployed, the Patriot system faced challenges in threat detection and engagement capabilities. The initial PAC-1 configuration, which focused primarily on aircraft threats, revealed limitations when confronting evolving missile threats. It struggled with false tracks and engagement reliability, sometimes leading to concerning outcomes like potential fratricide scenarios. Traditional military doctrine might have seen these as critical flaws requiring resolution before deployment. Instead, the program took a different approach: working with these imperfections to evolve the platform through the Post Deployment Build (PDB) concept.

Rather than pursuing flawless performance, the army implemented a series of evolutionary improvements, from PAC-2 with its enhanced missile defense capabilities to PAC-3 with its hit-to-kill technology. Each PDB iteration introduced new capabilities while addressing discovered limitations, creating a continuous improvement cycle that adapted to emerging threats.

The system's software architecture evolved through successive PDB updates, each building upon lessons learned from real-world operations. This iterative approach allowed us to rapidly integrate new capabilities while maintaining operational readiness. For instance, the transition from PAC-2 to PAC-3 wasn't just a missile upgrade—it represented a fundamental shift in engagement philosophy, moving from blast fragmentation to hit-to-kill technology.

Today, the Patriot remains a cornerstone of US and allied defense architecture precisely because it evolved through this approach of embracing imperfection. Each new PDB release and PAC configuration builds upon previous lessons learned, creating an increasingly capable system that adapts to emerging threats. Rather than waiting for perfect solutions, the program continuously evolved, allowing each iteration to inform the next stage of development.

The success of the Patriot program demonstrates a crucial principle: Progress comes through iteration, not perfection. In the SEAM framework, this principle is equally powerful. We recognize that perfection is not only unattainable but also undesirable. If you wait for a perfect solution, you'll never act. If you constantly dodge failure, your progress will be hindered. Instead, you act, assess, and modify—constantly improving as you go.

BUILDING ORGANIZATIONS THAT THRIVE ON IMPERFECTION

Creating organizations that can leverage imperfection requires a shift in how we think about success and failure. Instead of pursuing perfect execution, we need to build systems that can learn and adapt through imperfect iterations.

To achieve this, organizations need to develop:

- Flexible decision-making processes that can adapt to changing conditions
- Communication systems that value transparency about imperfections
- Training programs that emphasize adaptability over perfect execution
- Metrics that recognize the value of learning from imperfect outcomes

This means developing feedback mechanisms that capture and learn from deviations from the plan. It means creating cultures where experimentation is encouraged and failure is seen as valuable data rather than a catastrophe. Most importantly, it means recognizing that the most resilient systems are often those that maintain flexibility through controlled imperfection.

Based on my experience implementing these principles across military and civilian organizations, several key practices emerge:

1. Regular after-action reviews that focus on learning rather than blame
2. Cross-functional teams that bring together diverse perspectives and capabilities
3. Flexible resource allocation that can adapt to changing conditions
4. Leadership development that emphasizes adaptability and innovation
5. Recognition systems that reward creative problem-solving and effective adaptation

LEADERSHIP IN AN IMPERFECT WORLD

Building an organization that thrives on imperfection also takes the right kind of leadership.

Traditional leadership often focuses on eliminating imperfections through rigorous control and standardization. This approach stems from a fundamental misunderstanding of how complex systems work. In reality, the most effective leaders are those who understand that imperfection is not merely inevitable but can serve as a powerful catalyst for innovation and growth.

Leaders who insist on flawless execution and complete standardization often create systems that become brittle and inflexible. Their rigid approach eliminates room for adaptation, learning, and the natural variations that strengthen organizational resilience. This pursuit of perfection frequently leads to overcomplicated processes that break down under real-world conditions, ultimately creating more problems than they solve.

In contrast, leaders who embrace imperfection as a natural state create more robust and effective organizations. They understand the goal is not to eliminate every flaw but rather to build systems that can adapt and thrive because of their imperfections. These leaders focus on creating flexible frameworks that accommodate variation while maintaining core functionality.

By accepting that perfect solutions are neither possible nor desirable, leaders can foster environments where teams feel empowered to experiment, learn, and adapt. This approach creates a culture of continuous improvement rather than one paralyzed by pursuing unattainable perfection.

THE PATH FORWARD

Sometimes the most powerful lessons come from unexpected sources. As I mentioned in chapter 1, when my son Maddox was diagnosed with autism, Stacey and I faced a profound challenge to our assumptions about control and perfection. We initially resisted the unpredictability, clinging to routines and control. However, we eventually learned to embrace this "imperfection" as a unique aspect of our journey, adopting a more adaptive, SEAM-like approach to parenting. This experience, which I'll delve into later in the book, reshaped my understanding of leadership, strategy, and the importance of working with, rather than against, inherent imperfections in any system.

Back in the world of work, embracing imperfection doesn't mean abandoning standards or accepting poor performance. Rather, it means recognizing that the path to excellence often runs through imperfection. By building strategies and organizations that can learn from and adapt to imperfections, we create systems that are more resilient, innovative, and ultimately successful.

This understanding fundamentally changes how we approach:

- **Strategic planning**: Moving from rigid plans to adaptive frameworks
- **Leadership development**: Emphasizing flexibility and adaptation over control
- **Organizational design**: Creating structures that can learn and evolve
- **Performance measurement**: Developing metrics that value adaptation and learning
- **Innovation**: Embracing imperfect iterations as a path to breakthrough improvements

The next chapters will show how to put the principles of SEAM into action, building organizations that don't just survive uncertainty but harness it for competitive advantage. The true art of strategic leadership in an uncertain world lies not in achieving perfection but in learning to thrive within the reality of imperfection.

Chapter 4

STRATEGIZE—THE POWER OF PARTIAL FRAMING

"IN PREPARING FOR BATTLE, I HAVE ALWAYS FOUND THAT PLANS ARE USELESS, BUT PLANNING IS INDISPENSABLE."
—Dwight D. Eisenhower, *War in a Time of Peace*

The first phase of the SEAM framework—Strategize—represents a fundamental shift in how we approach planning. Traditional strategic planning often resembles building a fortress: rigid walls, controlled access points, and a design intended to resist change. But in today's environment, we need strategies that can grow and adapt like living organisms.

Over decades of experience across military service, defense strategy, business leadership, and community building, I have repeatedly witnessed the limitations of inflexible planning, when meticulously crafted strategies encounter unconsidered variables that no amount of preparation could have anticipated. Whether in combat operations, corporate ventures, or community initiatives, rigid protocols and unbending directives consistently proved less effective than adaptive approaches. The pursuit of a perfect execution often created greater challenges than the original problems we sought to solve. However, these moments of apparent failure became the most valuable catalysts for developing more resilient and effective approaches that could flex with real-world complexity.

THE TRADITIONAL VIEW OF STRATEGY

Strategy has deep historical roots. Military theorist Carl von Clausewitz defined it as "the use of engagements for the object of the war," while modern management scholar Michael Porter describes it as "creating a unique and valuable position, involving a different set of activities." Both definitions suggest intentional action toward specific goals, but they emerged in eras when change occurred more gradually than today.

Traditional strategic planning operates like architectural blueprints—detailed documents that specify how everything should fit together. This approach assumes we can accurately predict future conditions, control key variables, execute plans with minimal deviation, and achieve predetermined outcomes. Yet modern complexity regularly proves these assumptions wrong.

Consider Nokia's fall from mobile phone dominance. Their strategic planning was thorough and detailed, but their rigid framework couldn't adapt quickly enough to the

STRATEGIZE—THE POWER OF PARTIAL FRAMING

iPhone's revolutionary impact on consumer expectations. Nokia's engineers had developed touchscreen technology before Apple, but their strict strategic framework prevented them from bringing it to market effectively.

PARTIAL FRAMING: THE POWER OF THE OPEN SIDE

Imagine a picture frame. Traditional frames completely enclose their contents, defining rigid boundaries that don't allow input or adaptation. Most strategic models follow this pattern, attempting to frame every aspect of execution within strict parameters and minimize external influence.

But what happens when circumstances change? When new technologies emerge, customer preferences shift, or competitors make unexpected moves? Rigid frames often crack under pressure, leaving organizations scrambling to recover.

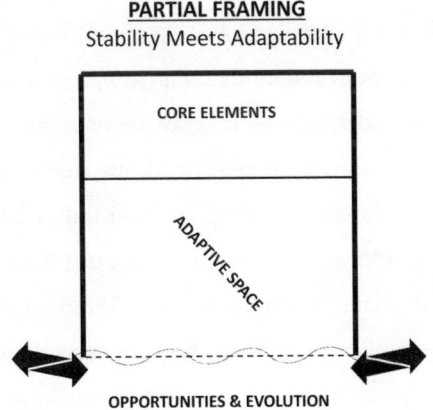

PARTIAL FRAMING
Stability Meets Adaptability

Partial framing is a sophisticated strategic approach that is frankly superior to traditional planning methodologies. By intentionally maintaining strategic ambiguity on one side of our conceptual framework, we create the opportunity for continuous organizational evolution while preserving core strategic intentions. In this way, partial framing goes beyond mere planning—it is an intelligent, nuanced design philosophy that embraces the inherent complexity and unpredictability of real-world systems.

Research in complex adaptive systems provides scientific validation for the partial framing approach. Studies show that systems characterized by both structural stability and adaptability consistently outperform both completely rigid and entirely fluid organizational models. This pattern mirrors natural evolutionary processes, where biological organisms maintain core functions while simultaneously developing sophisticated adaptive mechanisms.

The challenge lies in striking a balance between preserving essential organizational elements and allowing for flexible exploration and innovation. To achieve this balance, it's crucial to understand your organization's core competencies, values, and operational capabilities. Additionally, you must identify the areas where your organization needs to be adaptable and responsive to changing circumstances, which we can call "dynamic requirements." These requirements refer to the ability to adjust to shifting market conditions, emerging technologies, and evolving customer needs.

In my experience leading diverse military units, I've found that rigorous analysis of past successes and failures can help reveal the optimal balance between preservation and exploration. By examining what has worked well in the past and what hasn't, organizations can develop a deeper understanding of their strengths, weaknesses, and areas for improvement, ultimately informing their strategy for navigating complex and changing environments.

TWO PARTIAL FRAMING CASE STUDIES

Two examples, from the world of tech and the military, show the power of partial framing.

Adobe's Strategic Transformation

Adobe's transition from packaged software to cloud-based services shows the potency of partial framing in corporate strategy. After the 2008 recession caused its leaders to lay off 8 percent of its workforce, they wanted to avoid repeating such a move. So they set about creating a more futureproof foundation for the company. In 2013, Adobe made a bold strategic pivot by transforming its Creative Suite products into a subscription-based Creative Cloud model. Instead of trying to predict and control every detail of this transformation, Adobe created a strategic framework that maintained fundamental product quality, preserved customer relationships, and retained essential creative tools while introducing flexibility in pricing models and feature-delivery mechanisms.

This approach enabled Adobe to respond dynamically to market feedback. When customers initially resisted the subscription model, the company could strategically adjust pricing structures and implementation timelines without compromising its strategic vision. The results were extraordinary: Adobe's revenue grew from $4 billion in 2013 to over $12 billion in 2021, demonstrating the power of maintaining strategic direction while embracing adaptability.

Partial Framing in Military Operations

During my time with NATO in the United Kingdom, particularly through the turmoil of Brexit and the COVID-19 pandemic, partial framing proved an invaluable strategic tool. NATO's operational readiness relies on multinational exercises where allied forces cross national training boundaries to develop integrated tactics, collaborative techniques, and unified procedural approaches.

The pandemic created major challenges to these readiness initiatives. Travel restrictions, lockdowns, testing requirements, and quarantine protocols threatened to disrupt essential training events. However, by focusing on adaptive planning rather than rigid protocols, we found innovative ways to continue operations.

We worked with UK authorities to develop a framework

that balanced training requirements with rigorous health safety measures. Through careful site selection, social distancing, daily testing, and enhanced hygiene standards, we conducted a large-scale readiness exercise in early winter 2020, at the pandemic's peak.

This approach showed how we could maintain our core objectives while being flexible with implementation. We identified and preserved essential elements like training standards and force integration, while adapting our methodological approaches to meet pandemic challenges. As a result, we achieved our readiness goals with zero COVID-19 cases throughout the two-week exercise.

IMPLEMENTING PARTIAL FRAMING

Successful implementation of partial framing requires a systematic, rigorous approach. Organizations must examine their existing strategic frameworks to see which elements are essential and which could benefit from increased adaptability. This process frequently reveals historical instances where rigid planning generated missed opportunities or organizational constraints.

The methodology involves three main steps:
1. Identifying the nonnegotiable elements that define the organization's core identity and competitive advantage

2. Determining the areas where adaptability presents the most potential value
3. Establishing clear but flexible boundaries for adaptive exploration

As technological acceleration intensifies and systemic complexity increases, the capacity to create and navigate partial strategic frames becomes increasingly critical. Organizations that master this approach will be optimally positioned to seize emerging opportunities, navigate disruptive challenges, maintain competitive advantages, and drive sustainable innovation.

The future does not belong to those who plan with maximal rigidity, but to those who can maintain strategic coherence while adapting when circumstances evolve. Partial framing is a powerful instrument for achieving this delicate balance, enabling organizations to thrive amid uncertainty.

In the next chapter, we'll look more closely at the second component of the SEAM framework: Execution.

Chapter 5

EXECUTION— FROM PLAN TO IMPACT

"STRATEGY WITHOUT EXECUTION IS HALLUCINATION."
—Thomas Edison

A strategy, no matter how brilliant, remains merely words on paper until execution breathes life into it. I learned this lesson early in my military career when a seemingly perfect operational plan dissolved within minutes of first contact with the opposing force during a major training exercise. What saved us was not the plan itself, but our ability to execute flexibly and adapt rapidly as circumstances changed—kind of like the launch of Amazon Prime. When Jeff Bezos proposed offering unlimited two-day shipping for an annual fee, the execution challenges seemed massive: complex logistics, uncertain costs, and an unknown customer response. Yet Amazon succeeded not because they planned every detail perfectly, but because they built execution systems that could adapt and evolve as they learned.

Traditional execution often resembles a carefully

choreographed dance, where every step is planned and any deviation is considered a failure. However, real-world execution more closely resembles improvised jazz: there is a clear structure and direction, but success comes from how well you can adapt and innovate within that framework.

Building on the partial framing approach discussed in the previous chapter, this chapter explores how the SEAM framework approaches execution, transforming it from a rigid process into a flexible way to navigate uncertainty while maintaining strategic direction. Leaders can do so in three main ways: by embracing what I call proactive reactiveness, fighting momentum drag, and building agile execution systems.

PROACTIVE REACTIVENESS: THE ESSENCE OF EFFECTIVE EXECUTION

In military operations, success often depends on preparation, flexibility, and the ability to adapt to the unexpected. These principles also apply in our personal lives. When Maddox was diagnosed with autism at the age of five, my family and I were stationed overseas in the United Kingdom, navigating not just the complexities of military life but the sweeping disruptions caused by the COVID-19 pandemic.

The diagnosis arrived like a seismic shift, reframing our expectations and reshaping our family's routines. Maddox's autism came with newly emerging disruptive behaviors that we were just beginning to understand. COVID-19 amplified the challenges: Vaccines, homeschooling, social isolation, and being thousands of miles away from family and friends added layers of unpredictability to an already fragile situation. It was a storm of uncertainties, and through it, Stacey and I had to lean into proactive reactiveness.

Proactive reactiveness is a mindset, a way of navigating chaos that blends preparation with the ability to respond decisively in the moment. It rests on four core elements that work together in a continuous cycle: **predict**, **prepare**, **react**, and **adapt**.

The process begins with **prediction** not as mystical forecasting, but as intelligent anticipation based on deep understanding of your operational environment. **Preparation** follows, but not in the traditional sense of creating rigid response plans. Instead, you develop flexible resources and systems that can adapt to various scenarios. **Reaction** becomes necessary when change occurs, as it inevitably will. The key is making these reactions purposeful rather than panicked. **Adaptation** closes the loop, as you learn from each experience and adjust your approach accordingly.

Living overseas, far from our support system, required Stacey and I to predict potential hurdles before they escalated. Maddox's struggles with sensory overload became more pronounced during the isolation of COVID-19. Virtual schooling lacked the structure he needed, and the absence of familiar routines led to frequent outbursts and meltdowns.

Anticipating these triggers meant finding creative ways to recreate structure within the unstructured:

- Creating visual schedules
- Designing calming spaces at home
- Working with teachers to adapt learning strategies to Maddox's unique needs

Preparation became our lifeline. We immersed ourselves in learning about autism, connecting with online support groups, and leveraging whatever resources were available in a country where we didn't have the same access to services we might have had in the United States.

At home, we built a flexible yet structured environment to support both Maddox and his younger brother, Owen, who was just four at the time. The isolation of being overseas during a global pandemic pushed us to find new ways to connect not only as parents but as partners. We leaned on each other during moments of exhaustion, frustration, and doubt, and those moments shaped the resilience that held our family together.

This experience taught us a profound lesson: imperfection is not failure. It reinforced the principles discussed in earlier chapters about finding strength in apparent weaknesses. Proactive reactiveness is about embracing uncertainty, building adaptable systems, and maintaining forward momentum even when the path is unclear. In strategic execution, as in life, success comes not from having a perfect plan, but from developing the capacity to respond thoughtfully and creatively to unexpected challenges.

PROACTIVE REACTIVENESS
Anticipate and Adapt

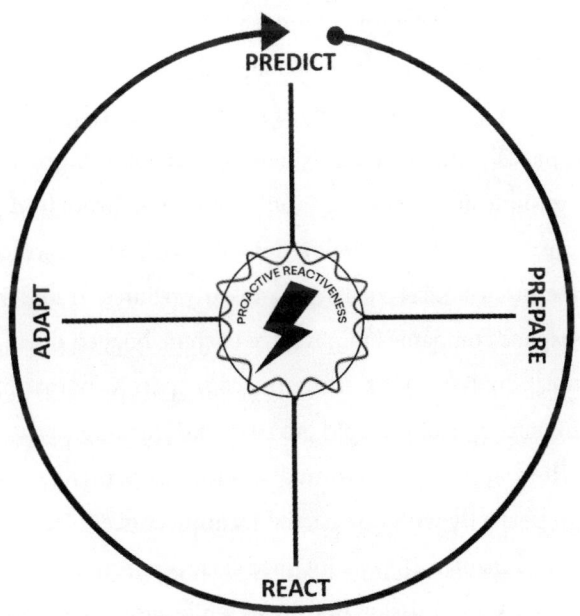

BREAKING THE MOMENTUM DRAG

One of the most insidious enemies of effective execution is what I call **momentum drag**: the gradual loss of energy and drive that can afflict even the most promising strategies. I witnessed this phenomenon repeatedly during large-scale military exercises, where initial enthusiasm would slowly give way to routine and rigidity.

Momentum drag often stems from disconnection between strategic intent and frontline execution. Teams lose sight of their role in the larger mission, resources become misaligned with priorities, and feedback loops break down. The result? Execution loses steam, and strategies stall. (Take most New Year's resolutions as a prime example!)

SpaceX, which we talked about in chapter 3, provides an example of overcoming momentum drag through adaptive execution. Their development of reusable rockets faced numerous technical challenges and early failures. Traditional aerospace companies might have become bogged down in endless analysis and testing. Instead, SpaceX maintained momentum through rapid iteration and learning.

Their approach embodied several key principles that align perfectly with our partial framing concept from the previous chapter. They maintained clear connection between daily work and mission objectives while allowing for rapid feedback loops from testing to development. Resources could be reallocated quickly based on immediate needs, and perhaps most importantly, they celebrated learning from failures rather than punishing them.

THE ARCHITECTURE OF AGILE EXECUTION

In the SEAM framework, successful execution is **agile**: able to respond to the unpredictability of a real-world environment. Through several examples from my military experience, I'll show what agile execution looks like on the ground, how leaders can better enable it, and how to measure the outcomes of this kind of approach.

Successful execution requires more than just flexibility; it demands structured adaptability. Like a complex neural network, organizational systems must maintain core connectivity while allowing for dynamic reconfiguration. During a critical global communication reform project, our team of twenty-five individuals from diverse military and civilian backgrounds confronted a challenge: transforming traditional hierarchical communication practices into a more responsive, interconnected system. With only one active-duty military member, we had to bridge cultural, technological, and procedural divides.

Our approach drew from multiple strategic principles: the principles of mission command from military doctrine, network-centric warfare concepts, and collaborative problem-solving methodologies. We created an execution framework that emphasized:

1. Shared cognitive space: establishing a common operational picture that transcended individual organizational boundaries.

2. Adaptive protocol design: developing communication interfaces that could accommodate diverse operational contexts while maintaining core strategic objectives.
3. Distributed decision-making: empowering team members to make critical choices within a broader strategic framework, reducing latency in complex decision environments.

The success of our approach hinged not on uniform compliance but on creating a flexible architecture that could accommodate diverse perspectives while maintaining strategic coherence.

Leading agile execution effectively requires a fundamental shift from traditional command-and-control approaches. I learned this lesson during a joint military exercise when communication systems failed, forcing unit commanders to make autonomous decisions based on their understanding of mission intent rather than detailed orders.

In this context, leaders act more as catalysts than commanders. They create conditions for success rather than trying to control every aspect of implementation. During my time as battery commander, this meant helping each team member understand how their specific role contributed to overall mission success.

When it comes to measurement, traditional metrics often fail to capture the true effectiveness of execution. When I led the test detachment at White Sands Missile Range, we developed a more nuanced approach to assessment that considered both quantitative and qualitative factors.

We measured adaptation speed—how quickly teams could adjust to new situations or requirements. We evaluated innovation within constraints, examining teams' ability to find creative solutions while maintaining strategic alignment. Resource efficiency became about optimal use of all available resources, not just cost control. Perhaps most importantly, we assessed team cohesion through the strength of coordination and shared understanding across the organization.

THE PATH TO EXECUTION EXCELLENCE

Effective execution isn't about perfect implementation of a plan, but about achieving results in an imperfect world. By embracing proactive reactiveness, fighting momentum drag, and building agile execution systems, you create the conditions for successful implementation even in uncertain environments.

In the next chapter, we'll explore how to assess execution effectiveness and make strategic adjustments based on real-world results. The key is maintaining momentum while learning and adapting, keeping your strategy relevant in an ever-changing world.

Chapter 6

ASSESSMENT— MEASURING SUCCESS

"IF YOU CAN'T MEASURE IT, YOU CAN'T IMPROVE IT."
— Peter Drucker

During my time leading missile defense operations, we faced a persistent challenge: How do you measure success when the enemy hasn't attacked? Traditional metrics like intercept rates in training exercises told only part of the story. The true measure of our effectiveness lay in our readiness to respond to threats that might never materialize, our ability to adapt to evolving capabilities, and our success in maintaining both equipment and personnel at peak performance.

This challenge mirrors the broader question facing every organization: How do you know your strategy is working? In the absence of real-time assessment, strategies often drift like ships without navigation systems, hoping they're heading in the right direction. But hope isn't a strategy, and measurement isn't just about collecting data—it's about creating feedback loops that guide strategic decisions.

THE EVOLUTION OF STRATEGIC ASSESSMENT

Traditional approaches to assessment often resembled an annual physical: scheduled, ritualistic, and too infrequent to catch problems early. Organizations would deploy strategies and wait months or years before evaluating outcomes. This delayed feedback loop created numerous problems, including missed opportunities for timely adjustments.

Here's an example from the nonprofit world. In 2021, the Patriot Bros. Association created a scholarship program for junior enlisted soldiers in the US Army Air Defense Artillery branch. Initially, we followed a traditional assessment model, focusing entirely on fundraising metrics and the number of scholarships we could offer. Our quarterly reviews centered on financial performance and donation targets. However, by concentrating solely on these metrics, we were overlooking crucial elements of program success.

When application season arrived, we faced a sobering reality. Despite having substantial funds available, we received only a handful of applications rather than the large pool of candidates we had anticipated. The delayed recognition of this issue highlighted a flaw in our assessment approach. We had waited too long to evaluate the broader picture of program effectiveness.

Instead, what we should have done was implement a more agile and comprehensive assessment approach, one that incorporated regular, real-time feedback and evaluation of multiple metrics, including program outreach, applicant engagement, and scholarship recipient outcomes. This would have allowed us to identify and address the issue of low application numbers earlier, potentially through adjustments to our marketing strategy, applicant outreach, or eligibility criteria.

This would have included monthly or bimonthly check-ins to monitor key performance indicators beyond financials (such as website traffic, social media engagement, and applicant feedback), as well as insights from stakeholders, including scholarship recipients, applicants, and partners.

This approach would have enabled data-driven decisions to adjust our strategy and optimize outcomes. By shifting from annual reviews to continuous evaluation, we could have avoided the surprise of low application numbers and made timely improvements. Our experience highlighted the importance of ongoing assessment, which we've since incorporated into our strategic planning process.

THE POWER OF CONTINUOUS DECISIVE ASSESSMENT

At the core of SEAM is **continuous decisive assessment**. Beyond simply gathering information, it's about making timely, impactful decisions based on that information. You don't just collect data for the sake of it, but to act on it. Assessments aren't just post-action evaluations, but ongoing, actionable steps that influence the strategy in real time.

The Three Levels of Continuous Decisive Assessment

This kind of assessment operates at three distinct but interconnected levels.

The first is **tactical assessment**, which focuses on immediate performance metrics and operational effectiveness. This is where you measure the day-to-day execution of your strategy. These metrics should be immediately actionable and tied to current operations.

Next is **operational assessment**, where you examine how different components of your strategy work together. This is where you identify and optimize the seams between different strategic elements. Operational assessment helps ensure that tactical successes translate into broader strategic achievements.

Third is **strategic assessment**, evaluating whether your organization is achieving its broader objectives and adapting effectively to change. This includes both quantitative metrics and qualitative evaluations of market position, competitive advantage, and long-term sustainability.

Building a Culture of Continuous Assessment

Creating an environment of continuous decisive assessment requires more than just implementing new metrics or buying better analytics tools. It requires thoughtful changes in how organizations think about and use information. Here's how to build that culture.

First, feedback should be timely and frequent, with

regular touchpoints where feedback is not just gathered but acted upon. Think of it as running sprints rather than a marathon. Regular checkpoints provide opportunities for teams to recalibrate, refocus, and make small but meaningful adjustments that keep them on track.

Next, teams should be empowered to act, with the autonomy to make real-time adjustments without waiting for endless approvals. They should be trusted to pivot based on the feedback they receive, ensuring that execution doesn't grind to a halt because of bottlenecked decision-making.

Leaders should also celebrate adjustments, not just outcomes. Too many organizations focus solely on the end result, ignoring the importance of the adjustments made along the way. In SEAM, the process of refinement is just as valuable as the final outcome. Celebrate teams that make timely pivots based on assessments, showing that flexibility is not a sign of weakness but strength.

Technology as an Assessment Enabler

Modern technology makes continuous assessment easier than ever. Tools like real-time analytics platforms and project management software help teams stay connected and up to date on performance metrics. However, it's essential to remember that technology is an enabler, not a solution.

The key is building assessment systems that:

- Filter signal from noise in the vast amount of available data

- Present information in actionable formats that enable quick decisions
- Support continuous learning and adaptation
- Enable rapid sharing of insights across the organization

CASE STUDY: CASA DI LEGNO DESIGN

My experience with the design firm I founded, Casa di Legno Design, illustrates the importance of continuous decisive assessment in identifying emerging opportunities. When I began creating social media marketing and graphic design content for my veteran nonprofit organization, the Patriot Bros. Association, I discovered an unexpected opportunity in the broader design market. If I had focused solely on traditional metrics like project completion and client satisfaction, I would have missed the larger market potential unfolding before me.

Drawing on my military background in systems assessment, I developed a comprehensive framework that evaluated five key dimensions:

1. Market sector adaptability—understanding how our design capabilities could flex to serve different market segments
2. Client portfolio diversification—ensuring we weren't overly dependent on any single client type

3. Design capability expansion—identifying areas where we needed to grow our technical skills
4. Cross-industry applications—recognizing how solutions developed for one sector could create opportunities in others
5. Innovation sustainability—ensuring our creative approaches remained fresh and relevant

This approach enabled us to identify and capitalize on opportunities before they became obvious to competitors. When our analysis showed increasing demand for specialized military organization branding, I tapped into my veteran community understanding to expand into morale patch design. This experience then opened doors to corporate logo design and web development and eventually led to high-profile aerospace projects including SpaceX rocket artwork.

LOOKING FORWARD: THE FUTURE OF STRATEGIC ASSESSMENT

Effective assessment isn't about perfect measurement; it's about creating feedback loops that enable better decisions and continuous improvement. The future of assessment lies in predictive analytics, integrated systems that break down silos between different assessment functions, and the ability to enable immediate response to changing conditions.

In the next chapter, we'll explore how to modify strategies based on assessment insights, completing the SEAM cycle of continuous improvement and adaptation.

Chapter 7

MODIFICATION—EMBRACING THE "SAME DIFFERENCE"

"IT IS NOT THE MOST INTELLECTUAL OF THE SPECIES THAT SURVIVES; IT IS NOT THE STRONGEST THAT SURVIVES; BUT THE SPECIES THAT SURVIVES IS THE ONE THAT IS ABLE BEST TO ADAPT AND ADJUST TO THE CHANGING ENVIRONMENT IN WHICH IT FINDS ITSELF."
—Leon Megginson

Effective assessment, as we explored in the previous chapter, often reveals the need for change. However, recognizing this need represents only the beginning. Strategic modification, perhaps the most challenging aspect of the SEAM framework, requires us to fundamentally transform our approach while maintaining our core purpose. As a father of a child with autism, I've come to understand the crucial distinction between adaptation, which merely adjusts existing processes, and modification, which fundamentally reimagines our approach while preserving core objectives.

BEYOND ADAPTATION: UNDERSTANDING STRATEGIC MODIFICATION

As you learned earlier, when Maddox received his autism diagnosis at age five, our world shifted dramatically. Before his diagnosis, he attended a general education classroom without any formal support structure. Like many parents, we initially tried to navigate the challenges through small adaptations to standard approaches. However, we quickly discovered that adaptation alone proved insufficient. We needed to shift our entire understanding of education, development, and success.

Our journey through different educational approaches illustrates this distinction perfectly. After Maddox's diagnosis, we moved from the general education setting to a self-contained classroom that offered specialized support and structure. When regression and behavioral inconsistencies emerged, we made another modification, transitioning to homeschooling. As his communication improved and he developed new skills, we returned to a general education setting but with a completely different approach and understanding than where we'd started.

Now, at age ten, Maddox's educational journey shows the power of strategic modification. Each transition represented not just an adaptation but a fundamental shift in how we approached his education. The goal remained constant—providing him with the best possible environment for learning and development—but our methods underwent complete reimagining.

The "Same Difference" Principle

The phrase "same difference" holds a special place in my heart, rooted in childhood memories with my father. As a kid, whenever I would misspeak and he would correct me, I'd often shrug and reply, "Same difference." My father would always challenge me with the same question: "How can something be the same and different at the same time?"

Years later, watching Maddox progress through his different educational settings, that childhood phrase took on new meaning. While our ultimate goals remained constant—helping our son develop, learn, and thrive—our methods required continuous and sometimes radical reimagining. Each educational setting demanded not just different tactics but an entirely new way of thinking about learning and development.

This childhood phrase had unknowingly captured a profound truth: Sometimes achieving the same objective requires embracing radically different approaches. What my father had questioned as a logical impossibility had become a powerful principle for navigating complex change.

Taking an Intelligent Approach to Modification

Through this journey, I learned to recognize when adaptation proves insufficient and fundamental modification becomes necessary. With Maddox, these moments often came when we noticed that despite our best efforts at adaptation, we weren't making meaningful progress. The signs weren't always dramatic; sometimes they appeared as subtle indicators that our current approach, despite continuous adjustment, wasn't serving his fundamental needs.

These experiences taught me to look for modification signals across three time horizons. First, immediate signals emerge when consistent effort yields diminishing returns. Second, medium-term indicators appear when environmental changes challenge current approaches. Finally, long-term signals surface when fundamental assumptions about success need rethinking.

Balancing Stability with Change

Strategic modification requires a structured approach that maintains stability while enabling fundamental change. With Maddox, we developed what I call the **modification matrix**: a framework for identifying core elements that must remain constant (like our commitment to his development), determining components that should change (like educational methods), managing transitions between approaches, and monitoring effectiveness.

This matrix helped us maintain consistency in our core mission of supporting Maddox's growth and development while radically reimagining how to achieve it. Each educational transition became not just a change of setting but a careful modification of our entire approach to learning and development.

Therein lies the key to successful modification: understanding that change and continuity function as complementary forces that must remain balanced. Through Maddox's journey, we learned that the most successful modifications maintained clear connections to our fundamental purpose while reimagining how to achieve it.

This approach requires developing what I call modification intelligence: the ability to recognize when adaptation proves insufficient and modification becomes necessary. It involves cultivating both the courage to make fundamental changes and the wisdom to preserve essential elements that give meaning and direction to your efforts.

The Human Element

Perhaps the most challenging aspect of strategic modification involves managing the human dimension of change. With Maddox, we discovered that new educational approaches meant little without addressing the emotional and psychological factors involved. Success required creating an environment where everyone—Maddox, his brother Owen, Stacey, and I—felt secure enough to embrace fundamental change while maintaining our family's core values and connections.

This led us to develop a more nuanced approach to modification, one that recognized the importance of narrative in helping everyone understand and embrace change. We learned to frame modifications not as departures from our goals but as steps in pursuing them, another manifestation of the "same difference" principle.

THE BRIDGE TO STRATEGIC ALIGNMENT

Successful change requires more than just recognizing when and how to modify strategy. It demands a deep understanding of how to maintain alignment between goals, methods, and resources throughout the modification process. This alignment challenge becomes particularly crucial during periods of significant change, when the risk of disconnection between strategic intent and operational reality is highest.

The process of strategic modification never truly ends; it continues as a process of evolution and refinement. Through Maddox's continuing journey, we constantly remember that the most powerful modifications often come not from changing our destinations but from fundamentally reimagining our paths to reaching them.

In the next chapter, we will explore how all elements of the SEAM framework—Strategy, Execution, Assessment, and Modification—work together to create organizations and approaches that don't just survive change but thrive on it. The key lies not in perfecting any single element but in maintaining dynamic harmony between them all.

Chapter 8

STRATEGIC HARMONY— ALIGNING GOALS, METHODS, AND RESOURCES

> **"STRATEGY WITHOUT TACTICS IS THE SLOWEST ROUTE TO VICTORY. TACTICS WITHOUT STRATEGY IS THE NOISE BEFORE DEFEAT."**
> —Sun Tzu

In late 2018, I stood in a command center in Qatar, staring at a map that showed the disposition of air defense forces across the Middle East. After nearly two decades of focusing primarily on Iraq and Afghanistan, the US military was pivoting toward great-power competition. This shift demanded a fundamental realignment of our air defense capabilities not just in terms of physical assets, but in how we thought about regional security itself.

The challenge before us loomed large: How do you realign strategic assets globally while maintaining regional security in an area still fraught with tension? This wasn't simply about moving Patriot batteries around on a map. It required rethinking the entire concept of integrated air defense in the Gulf Cooperation Council region, transitioning from a US-centric model to one that leveraged host nation capabilities more effectively.

This experience would teach me profound lessons about strategic alignment that apply far beyond military operations—lessons about how organizations of any type can align their goals, methods, and resources to achieve strategic harmony.

UNDERSTANDING STRATEGIC HARMONY

Strategic harmony occurs when an organization's goals (ends), methods (ways), and resources (means) work together like a well-conducted orchestra. Each element plays its part while contributing to a greater whole. But achieving this harmony demands more complexity than simply ensuring everything matches on paper.

Our situation in the Middle East illustrated this complexity. Our goal seemed clear: maintain regional air defense capabilities while freeing up strategic assets for global requirements. Our methods involved greater reliance on host nation defenses and enhanced integration of regional air defense networks. Our resources included not just physical assets like Patriot batteries, but relationships with partner nations, training capabilities, and technical integration systems.

The challenge lies in aligning these elements in a way that worked. Previous attempts at regional integrated air defense had often faltered not because of technical limitations, but because of misalignment between political goals, operational methods, and available resources.

Through this experience and others throughout my career, I've identified three critical dimensions of alignment that organizations must master:

- **Vertical alignment**, connecting strategic goals to tactical actions. In the Middle East, this meant ensuring that every training exercise, system integration effort, and diplomatic engagement served our strategic objectives.
- **Horizontal alignment**, coordinating across different organizational units. For us, this involved synchronizing efforts between different military commands, US government agencies, and partner nations.
- **Temporal alignment**, maintaining consistency over time while enabling evolution. This proved crucial as we implemented changes that would take years to fully realize.

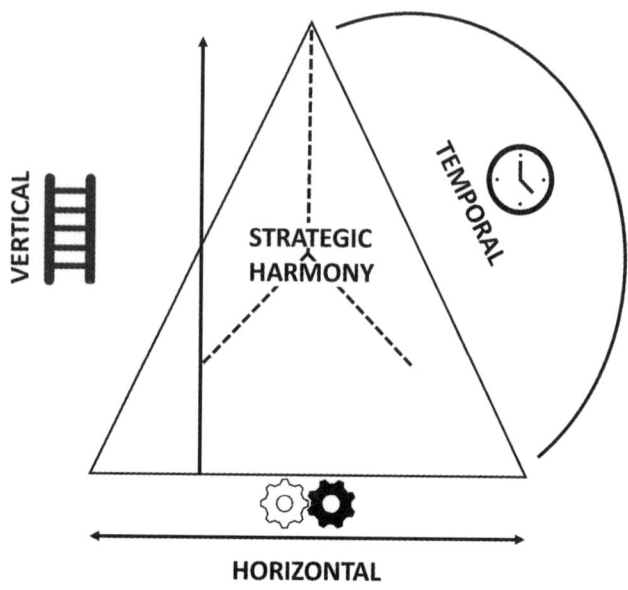

CASE STUDY: THE REGIONAL INTEGRATED AIR DEFENSE EVOLUTION

Our experience with regional air defense integration in the Gulf Cooperation Council (GCC) region provided a perfect laboratory for understanding the complex relationship between strategic goals, methods, and resources. Looking back, this initiative helped shape my understanding of how these elements must align for strategic success.

The ends seemed clear at first: maintain robust regional air defense while creating flexibility for global force posture

STRATEGIC HARMONY—ALIGNING GOALS, METHODS, AND RESOURCES

adjustments. Several GCC nations, including Saudi Arabia, the United Arab Emirates, Kuwait, Bahrain, and Qatar, had acquired advanced air defense capabilities through Foreign Military Sales. This presented an opportunity to reimagine regional defense, but it required aligning the ends, ways, and means.

Ends (Strategic Goals):

- Maintain effective regional air defense coverage
- Enable US force posture flexibility
- Build sustainable partner capacity
- Ensure collective regional security

Ways (Methods):

- Integration of national air defense systems
- Standardized training and procedures
- Coordinated response protocols
- Information-sharing mechanisms

Means (Resources):

- Partner-nation Patriot and THAAD systems
- US technical expertise and support
- Training facilities and capabilities
- Existing relationships and partnerships

This initiative clearly showed us the interdependencies between ends, ways, and means. We quickly learned that misalignment in any area could undermine the entire effort.

For instance, our initial goal of rapid integration (ends) didn't align with available training capacity (means) or existing procedural differences (ways).

Here's what we learned about strategic alignment through this experience:

Resources shape reality. We learned to start by understanding available means rather than ideal ends. Partner capabilities, training capacity, and political will defined what was possible more than our strategic vision.

Methods must bridge the gap. The ways we chose had to realistically connect our available means to desired ends. This often meant developing new approaches that could work within existing constraints rather than pursuing ideal but impractical solutions.

Goals require flexibility. Sometimes we needed to modify our ends based on the reality of our means and the effectiveness of our ways. This taught me the importance of what would later become SEAM's concept of partial framing.

But perhaps our most valuable insight came from understanding how **cultural factors** influenced all three elements: Different nations had varying strategic objectives and risk tolerances (ends), national approaches to air defense operations (ways) varied significantly, and even the definition of available resources (means) differed across cultures.

Ensuring the sustainability of our strategic alignment efforts therefore required:

- **Clear vision translation**: Ensuring everyone

understood not just what we were doing (ways) and what we had to work with (means), but why we were doing it (ends)
- **Flexible integration frameworks**: Creating structures that could accommodate different national capabilities and approaches while maintaining strategic coherence
- **Resource optimization**: Learning to leverage existing capabilities and relationships rather than trying to create perfect but unsustainable solutions

Looking back on this experience, it's clear that alignment requires constant and simultaneous attention to ends, ways, and means simultaneously, recognition of cultural and human factors, willingness to adjust goals to match reality rather than just seeking more resources, and an understanding that the connections between elements matter as much as the elements themselves.

Leaders of course play a crucial role in creating and maintaining strategic alignment. First, they must be **vision translators**, able to make strategic goals meaningful at all levels of the organization. In the Middle East, this meant helping every participant from senior commanders to individual operators understand how their role contributed to the larger mission. They must also be effective **resource stewards**, balancing competing demands for limited resources while maintaining strategic focus. This requires both careful planning and the courage to make difficult trade-offs. Last but not least, they need systems for continuously **monitoring alignment** across all dimensions. In our case, this included regular assessments of both technical integration and partnership effectiveness.

THE PATH TO STRATEGIC HARMONY

As organizations face increasing complexity and change, maintaining strategic alignment becomes more challenging. Successful strategic alignment requires constant attention to the relationship between goals, methods, and resources, along with the flexibility to adjust as conditions change.

Our experiences in realigning air defense capabilities in the Middle East demonstrated that effective alignment demands both rigorous systems and human understanding. It requires leaders who can think systematically while remaining attuned to the human factors that ultimately determine success. And it means building organizations that can adapt while maintaining alignment—what I call dynamic alignment capabilities, or the organizational muscles that allow for continuous adjustment while maintaining strategic coherence. In our case, this meant developing capabilities for rapid assessment, flexible response, continuous learning, and relationship maintenance through change.

In the next chapter, we'll explore how organizations can

navigate risk in an uncertain world, building on the foundation of strategic alignment to create resilient and adaptive strategies.

Chapter 9

NAVIGATING RISK IN AN UNCERTAIN WORLD

"IF YOU DON'T INVEST IN RISK MANAGEMENT, IT DOESN'T MATTER WHAT BUSINESS YOU'RE IN, IT'S A RISKY BUSINESS."
—Gary Cohn

You might think the riskiest decisions I've faced involved missile defense or military operations. But try this one: With twelve months left until military retirement, I decided to write a book. Now, add in running a growing graphic design LLC, serving as president of the Patriot Bros. Association, maintaining advisory roles on multiple boards, and—oh yes, moving my entire family from Virginia to Alabama during the holiday season. In two weeks. If that's not a master class in risk management, I don't know what is.

This chapter explores how organizations navigate risk in an increasingly uncertain world. But instead of focusing solely on corporate or military examples, let me share how the principles of risk management played out in my own

UNDERSTANDING RISK IN COMPLEX ENVIRONMENTS

strategic juggling act of roles, responsibilities, and major life transitions.

UNDERSTANDING RISK IN COMPLEX ENVIRONMENTS

Risk isn't just about threat assessment and mitigation anymore. Sometimes it's about staring at a blank Word document at 2:00 a.m., wondering if anyone will read your thoughts on strategic seams while your design client needs logos by morning, three board meetings loom tomorrow, and retirement paperwork sits half-finished on your desk. In today's interconnected world, risks cascade across systems in ways that can be difficult to predict or control.

Since we're talking about risk management, I'm going to share some actual risk assessments from my current juggling act. And yes, I'm taking a risk by breaking from traditional chapter format, but what better way to demonstrate risk management than by taking one?

> **STRATEGIC RISK ASSESSMENT MATRIX #1:**
> **THE DAILY PARENT TIME DILEMMA**
>
> **Risk:** Missing Kids' Evening FaceTime While at Board Meeting
> **Probability:** High (4/5)
> **Impact:** Severe (4/5)
> **Mitigation:** Prescheduled backup time slots, extra weekend trampoline sessions
>
> **Risk:** Poor Internet During Parent-Teacher Meeting
> **Probability:** Medium (3/5)
> **Impact:** Moderate (3/5)
> **Mitigation:** Multiple devices ready, backup hotspot, strategically positioned tablet
>
> **Risk:** Work Call During Promised Play Time
> **Probability:** High (4/5)
> **Impact:** Critical (5/5)
> **Mitigation:** Strict calendar blocking, designated "no meeting" windows

You might laugh, but these assessments are as crucial as any military operation planning. When you're trying to maintain strong family connections while geographically separated, every moment counts.

THE GREAT JUGGLING ACT: A STUDY IN CASCADING RISK

> ### STRATEGIC RISK ASSESSMENT MATRIX #2: THE BOOK-WRITING ADVENTURE
>
> **Risk:** Falling Asleep at Keyboard at 2:00 a.m.
> **Probability:** Certain (5/5)
> **Impact:** Chapter Makes No Sense (4/5)
> **Mitigation:** Strategic coffee deployment, voice recordings during commute
>
> **Risk:** Missing Design Client Deadline Due to Writing
> **Probability:** Medium (3/5)
> **Impact:** Revenue Impact (4/5)
> **Mitigation:** Time blocking, parallel processing, energy drinks
>
> **Risk:** Publisher Deadline Collision with Military Duties
> **Probability:** High (4/5)
> **Impact:** Severe (4/5)
> **Mitigation:** Leave planning, weekend writing sprints, understanding supervisor

Picture this risk portfolio:

Professional Risks:

- Making a military career transition after two decades of service

- Growing a graphic design business during a crucial period
- Leading a nonprofit organization's expanding initiatives
- Maintaining multiple board commitments
- Writing a book that may or may not find its audience

Personal Risks:
- Moving my family across states during the holidays
- Becoming a geographic bachelor to maintain commitments
- Balancing family time with multiple professional roles
- Managing the transition from military to civilian life

Financial Risks:
- Investing in hybrid publishing
- Purchasing a home in a new state
- Supporting my family through geographic separation
- Building multiple income streams for post-retirement

Sounds like a recipe for disaster, right? Not with SEAM in my back pocket. The framework proved invaluable in managing this complex risk environment; here's how I put it to good use:

- **Strategize:** Instead of trying to eliminate risks, I identified which ones served long-term goals.

Writing a book while running multiple ventures? Worth it. Moving during the holidays? Necessary for family stability.
- **Execute:** Implementation required ruthless prioritization and efficient systems. Each role needed clear boundaries and dedicated time.
- **Assess:** Continuous feedback from family, clients, team members, and my own energy levels guided adjustments.
- **Modify:** Plans evolved constantly, from book-writing schedules to business operations to family arrangements.

FROM STATIC DEFENSE TO DYNAMIC NAVIGATION

Traditional risk management often resembles a game of Whac-A-Mole. But try playing Whac-A-Mole while designing logos, leading nonprofit initiatives, attending board meetings, preparing for military retirement, and writing a book. You quickly learn to develop what I call **dynamic risk navigation**—a complex balancing act across four dimensions of risk:
- **Strategic**: Beyond just writing a book or running a business, the real strategic risk lay in ensuring all these different roles would create a coherent post-military career path rather than just a collection of activities.

- **Operational**: How do you effectively operate as a military officer, business owner, nonprofit leader, board member, author, and family man simultaneously? The answer involves precise time management, clear priorities, and a very understanding family.
- **External**: External risks came from every direction: market uncertainties, publishing industry dynamics, military transition timelines, and yes, even housing market conditions in Alabama.
- **Emergent**: The unexpected interactions between different roles created their own challenges. A nonprofit event might conflict with a client deadline, or a board meeting might overlap with crucial family time.

Creating effective risk management systems also required rethinking how I approached every role. In my military life, this meant creating a clear transition timeline and delegating noncritical tasks so I could focus on my essential responsibilities. In business operations, it meant systematizing project management, managing client expectations, and creating scalable design processes. In my nonprofit leadership role, I needed to focus on strong team development, clear organizational systems, and delegating authority. For my board commitments, it meant participating strategically, being efficient with meetings, and contributing in ways I could add the most value. And in my family life, I focused on protecting family time, establishing clear lines of communication, and sharing decision-making.

THE FAMILY CONNECTION CHALLENGE

Speaking of family, as I navigated the complexities of my personal and professional life, I realized that maintaining strong family connections was not just a matter of scheduling regular video calls or planning occasional visits. It required a deliberate approach to managing risk, one that considered the multiple dimensions of risk that impacted our family's well-being.

I began by identifying the strategic risks that threatened our family's cohesion, such as the potential impact of my military career transition on our family's stability and security. I also considered the operational risks, such as the challenges of managing my time and priorities across multiple roles and responsibilities. Then there were external risks, such as the uncertainty of the housing market or the demands of my nonprofit leadership role.

But it was the emergent risks that proved the most challenging. The unexpected interactions between my different roles and responsibilities created unanticipated conflicts and challenges.

To mitigate these risks and maintain strong family connections, I used the four dimensions of risk to develop a matrix that helped me visualize and manage the relationship between my different roles and responsibilities.

- The **strategic** dimension helped me ensure that all my different roles and responsibilities aligned with my long-term goals and vision for our family.
- The **operational** dimension enabled me to manage my time and priorities effectively, ensuring that I was able to fulfill my family responsibilities.
- The **external** dimension allowed me to anticipate and prepare for external risks and challenges that might impact our family's well-being.
- The **emergent** dimension helped me identify and mitigate the unexpected interactions and conflicts that arose between my different roles and responsibilities.

The matrix helped me prioritize my time and energy, manage risk, and make intentional decisions that aligned with our family's values and goals.

STRATEGIC RISK ASSESSMENT MATRIX #3: GEOGRAPHIC BACHELOR LIFE

Risk: Kids Growing Too Fast During Separation
Probability: Certain (5/5)
Impact: Heart Wrenching (5/5)
Mitigation: Daily FaceTime, surprise visits, shared online activities

Risk: Missing Important Appointments
Probability: Medium (3/5)
Impact: High (4/5)
Mitigation: Shared digital calendar with Stacey, remote participation when possible

Risk: Trampoline Skills Getting Rusty
Probability: Low (2/5)
Impact: Dad Reputation Damage (3/5)
Mitigation: Intensive bounce sessions during visits, regular practice videos

TECHNOLOGY AND RISK MANAGEMENT

Modern technology transformed how I managed these multiple roles. Project management software, digital design tools, virtual meeting platforms, and cloud storage became critical risk management tools.

STRATEGIC RISK ASSESSMENT MATRIX #4
THE DIGITAL FAMILY CONNECTION

Risk: FaceTime Technical Issues During Story Time
Probability: Medium (3/5)
Impact: Bedtime Disruption (4/5)
Mitigation: Multiple backup devices, prerecorded stories for emergencies

> **Risk:** Missing Important School Updates
> **Probability:** Low (2/5)
> **Impact:** High (4/5)
> **Mitigation:** Triple redundant notification systems, daily check-ins with Stacey
>
> **Risk:** Calendar Sync Failures
> **Probability:** Medium (3/5)
> **Impact:** Critical (5/5)
> **Mitigation:** Multiple calendar systems, weekly family planning calls

THE ULTIMATE RISK MATRIX

The most successful organizations and individuals don't just survive uncertainty; they learn to thrive on it. Even if that means tracking family commitments across three time zones while writing about strategic management between trampoline sessions and FaceTime calls.

As we move into our discussion of technology's role in strategy, remember that sometimes the biggest risk is not taking one at all. Whether that's writing a book, moving your family across the country, or including risk assessment matrices in your chapter about risk assessment.

> **FINAL RISK ASSESSMENT**
> **WRITING A BOOK ABOUT RISK WHILE LIVING IT**
>
> **Risk:** Readers Finding These Matrices Amusing
> **Probability:** High (4/5)
> **Impact:** Mission Success (5/5)
> **Desired Outcome:** Demonstrating that risk management is universal
>
> **Risk:** Traditional Publishers Questioning Format
> **Probability:** Certain (5/5)
> **Impact:** Worth It (5/5)
> **Mitigation:** You're reading this, aren't you?

Chapter 10

HARNESSING TECHNOLOGY FOR STRATEGIC ADVANTAGE

> "THE REAL PROBLEM OF HUMANITY IS THE FOLLOWING: WE HAVE PALEOLITHIC EMOTIONS, MEDIEVAL INSTITUTIONS, AND GODLIKE TECHNOLOGY."
> — Edward O. Wilson

If navigating risk in today's world feels like juggling flaming torches, technology is the fire-resistant glove that keeps you from getting burned. Just as careful risk management allows us to navigate uncertainty, technology amplifies our ability to strategize, execute, assess, and modify, turning chaos into opportunity.

In this chapter, we'll explore how the SEAM framework thrives when paired with the right tools. By examining how technology supports each phase, we'll uncover its power to enhance decision-making, streamline operations, and enable continuous improvement.

STRATEGIC PLANNING: TURNING DATA INTO DECISIONS

Effective strategic planning starts with understanding, and technology can help provide the necessary clarity. Gone are the days when intuition and gut feelings alone guided strategy. With advanced data analytics, scenario modeling, and collaboration tools, leaders can make decisions rooted in real-time insights rather than assumptions.

Data-Driven Insights

Risk management taught us the importance of assessing cascading threats. Technology now gives us the ability to predict them. Platforms like Tableau and Power BI transform raw data into actionable insights, enabling leaders to spot trends and opportunities before they fully emerge.

In the military, this might mean leveraging battlefield intelligence to predict enemy actions. In business, it could mean more precisely understanding customer behavior and market dynamics.

Smarter Scenario Planning

Technology enhances scenario planning by simulating potential outcomes with predictive analytics tools. Programs like Anaplan allow organizations to model risks, opportunities, and outcomes across different variables, whether it's a business expansion or a military maneuver.

Predictive analytics doesn't eliminate uncertainty, but can help transform it into foresight. Leaders can plan for the unexpected, refining their strategies based on a clearer understanding of what's likely to happen.

Easier Global Collaboration

Strategic planning in the digital age is no longer bound by geography. Collaboration platforms like Zoom, Microsoft Teams, and Slack let teams work together easily, whether they're across town or across continents. These tools democratize input, allowing diverse perspectives to enrich the planning process.

EXECUTION: FROM VISION TO REALITY

In the SEAM framework, execution is where strategies come alive. Technology ensures those strategies move from paper to practice with speed, precision, and adaptability.

Automation for Efficiency

Automation tools reduce the burden of repetitive tasks, freeing human resources for higher-value activities. Whether it's supply chain operations or customer interactions, automation streamlines execution. For example, AI-driven tools like chatbots handle routine queries, while logistics systems automatically optimize delivery schedules.

Project Management Tools

Executing complex strategies without a clear structure invites disaster. Platforms like Asana and Monday.com simplify task management, ensuring that every team member knows what needs to be done, when, and by whom.

For military operations, this means synchronized efforts across units. For businesses, it means staying on track and on budget, even when the unexpected arises.

Streamlined Supply Chains

In military and civilian contexts alike, supply chain management tools ensure resources get where they need to be. Real-time tracking, automated demand forecasting, and optimized delivery routes help reduce inefficiencies, keeping operations smooth under pressure.

ASSESSMENT: CONTINUOUS IMPROVEMENT IN REAL TIME

In chapter 9, we explored the necessity of reassessment in dynamic environments. Technology enhances this process, providing leaders with tools to evaluate strategies as they unfold.

Real-Time Dashboards

Dashboards powered by analytics provide live updates on key metrics. Whether it's operational efficiency, financial performance, or mission success, these dashboards enable leaders to adjust strategies dynamically.

Feedback Loops
Feedback systems collect data from customers, employees, or the field, ensuring that assessment isn't a onetime event but an ongoing process. The military uses after-action reports; businesses use real-time customer reviews. Both rely on feedback to refine their next steps.

MODIFICATION: ADAPTING WITH PRECISION

Adapting strategy in real time requires flexibility and speed, and technology provides both.

Cloud Scalability
Cloud-based platforms let organizations pivot quickly. Need to adjust your strategy for a new market or battlefield? Cloud technology can help you implement changes more quickly and effectively across teams.

Simulation and Testing
Before committing to major changes, simulation tools let leaders model the impact of modifications. This reduces the risk of unintended consequences and ensures changes are well informed.

SCALING GREAT STRATEGY WITH TECHNOLOGY

When integrated effectively, technology becomes a strategic multiplier, enhancing every aspect of the SEAM framework. It equips leaders to navigate uncertainty, optimize operations, and adapt quickly to changing conditions.

It's crucial to remember, though, that technology is a tool, not a replacement for leadership and vision. As Steve Jobs said, "Technology only amplifies true leadership." Even the most advanced and exciting technology requires strategic intent to be effective. Leaders must integrate it thoughtfully, ensuring that human judgment remains the driving force.

As we transition to the next chapter, we'll move from theory to practice, exploring case studies and real-world applications of the SEAM framework. From military operations to retail businesses, these examples will demonstrate the power of embracing imperfection while navigating the complexities of modern strategy.

Chapter 11

SEAM IN ACTION: CASE STUDIES AND REAL-WORLD INSIGHTS

"EXPERIENCE IS THE TEACHER OF ALL THINGS."
—Julius Caesar

Theory becomes meaningful when tested against reality. Throughout this book, we've explored the components of the SEAM framework: how to strategize with partial framing, execute with flexibility, assess continuously, and modify with purpose. Now we'll examine three cases that demonstrate both the power of these principles and the cost of ignoring them.

THE AFGHANISTAN CAMPAIGN: A STUDY IN STRATEGIC EVOLUTION

The US military's involvement in Afghanistan spanned nearly two decades, evolving from a focused counterterrorism mission into a complex nation-building effort. This transformation offers insights into the challenges of maintaining strategic coherence during prolonged operations.

In the immediate aftermath of 9/11, the mission was clear: disrupt Al Qaeda and prevent Afghanistan from serving as a terrorist haven. The initial military campaign demonstrated remarkable effectiveness, combining special operations forces, air power, and local allies to achieve rapid tactical success.

However, as the mission expanded to include counterinsurgency and nation building, the clarity of purpose began to blur. What started as a focused military operation evolved into a complex effort involving multiple agencies, international partners, and competing objectives.

Through the lens of the SEAM framework, several critical issues emerge:

- **Strategic partial framing**: The initial strategy failed to create appropriate space for evolution. Instead of maintaining flexible strategic boundaries that could accommodate changing conditions, each new challenge led to mission expansion without clear limits.
- **Execution challenges**: The military demonstrated tactical adaptability, developing new counterinsurgency techniques and building partner capacity. However, these tactical successes often masked strategic drift. Units rotated through the theater, each implementing their own interpretation of the mission, creating a patchwork of efforts rather than coherent progress.

- **Assessment failures**: Metrics focused heavily on tactical outputs (troops trained, areas secured, projects completed) rather than strategic outcomes. This led to what military analysts call "successes without victory," where individual achievements failed to generate strategic progress.
- **Modification struggles**: When modifications did occur, they often represented reactions to immediate challenges rather than strategic reorientations. The surge of 2009, for example, addressed tactical challenges but did not resolve the fundamental strategic questions that persisted.

The Afghanistan experience reveals several crucial insights:
- Clear strategic boundaries matter more than detailed plans.
- Tactical success doesn't guarantee strategic progress.
- Assessment must focus on outcomes, not just outputs.
- Modifications need to address root causes, not just symptoms.

THE F35 JOINT STRIKE FIGHTER: COMPLEXITY AND ADAPTATION

The F35 program represents one of the most ambitious

defense acquisition efforts in history. Its goal of creating a common fighter platform for multiple services and international partners perfectly illustrates the challenges of managing complex strategic initiatives.

The program's original concept was compelling: develop a common aircraft platform that could be adapted for different service requirements, reducing costs through economies of scale while maintaining advanced capabilities. However, the reality proved far more complex.

Early development faced significant challenges:

- Technical integration issues between different systems
- Cost overruns and schedule delays
- Competing requirements from different services
- Complex international partnerships

The program's eventual progress emerged through what effectively became a SEAM-like approach, though not explicitly framed as such:

- **Strategic adaptation**: The program shifted from seeking perfect commonality to accepting necessary variations, focusing on managing rather than eliminating differences between variants.
- **Execution flexibility**: Development and testing procedures evolved to allow concurrent progress on different aspects of the program rather than requiring sequential completion.

- **Continuous assessment**: The program established more robust feedback mechanisms between testing, development,, and operational units, allowing faster identification and resolution of issues.
- **Modification integration**: Rather than waiting for perfect solutions, the program adopted a continuous improvement approach, incorporating upgrades and modifications throughout the development cycle.

The F35 experience demonstrates how complex programs can benefit from SEAM principles:

- Accept and manage complexity rather than trying to eliminate it.
- Build feedback mechanisms into development processes.
- Allow for concurrent progress on different program elements.
- Maintain focus on core requirements while managing variations.

BLOCKBUSTER: OBSOLESCENCE AS THE COST OF STRATEGIC RIGIDITY

Blockbuster's fall from market dominance to bankruptcy offers a stark lesson in the importance of strategic adaptability. Their story illustrates how even strong market positions can erode when organizations fail to evolve with their environment.

At its peak, Blockbuster dominated video rental with thousands of stores and strong brand recognition. However, several critical strategic failures led to their decline:

- **Market misreading**: Blockbuster saw itself in the retail rental business rather than the entertainment access business, missing the significance of emerging digital distribution models.
- **Resource lock-in**: Heavy investment in physical infrastructure created resistance to business model changes that might threaten existing assets.
- **Cultural inflexibility**: A culture built around retail operations struggled to embrace digital innovation and changing customer preferences.

Analyzing Blockbuster's decline through our framework reveals several missed opportunities:

- **Strategic framing**: Rather than creating space for evolution in their strategy, Blockbuster remained rigidly focused on their existing business model. They needed partial framing that maintained core strengths while allowing for new approaches.
- **Execution failures**: When they did attempt to enter new markets, execution lacked commitment and consistency. Their online efforts often seemed designed to protect the existing business rather than build new capabilities.

- **Assessment blindness**: They continued measuring success through traditional retail metrics even as the market shifted toward digital consumption. This prevented them from recognizing the speed and significance of market changes.
- **Modification resistance**: When modifications did occur, they were often too late and too limited. Their eventual attempt to eliminate late fees, for example, came years after this pain point had driven customers to seek alternatives.

Blockbuster's experience offers crucial insights for modern organizations:

- Business model innovation must be proactive, not reactive.
- Core competencies can become core rigidities if not regularly reassessed.
- Market leadership requires constant evolution, not just optimization.
- Customer relationships must drive strategy, not protect existing assets.

COMMON THREADS AND KEY LESSONS

These three cases, spanning military operations, defense acquisition, and corporate strategy, reveal several universal principles about strategic success in complex environments.

First, they show the power of **partial framing**. Success requires maintaining clear direction while creating space for evolution. Whether in military operations, product development, or business strategy, rigid frameworks often fail in dynamic environments.

They also reveal the importance of **continuous decisive assessment**. Organizations must develop robust feedback mechanisms that connect strategic intent with operational reality. Assessment needs to focus on meaningful outcomes rather than just easily measured outputs.

And they show the critical role of **timely modification**. Successful organizations modify strategies based on emerging realities rather than waiting for crises to force change. This requires both the capability to change and the wisdom to know when change becomes necessary.

As we move into our final chapter, these cases remind us that strategic success requires more than good theories or detailed plans. It demands the ability to navigate complexity while maintaining coherence, to adapt while preserving purpose, and to learn while continuing to execute.

The challenges faced by the organizations in this chapter mirror those that all modern organizations face: increasing complexity, rapid change, and the need for continuous adaptation. The SEAM framework offers not just a theoretical approach but a practical way to navigate these challenges while maintaining strategic effectiveness.

Chapter 12

SHAPING THE FUTURE OF STRATEGY WITH SEAM

"THE BEST WAY TO PREDICT THE FUTURE IS TO CREATE IT."
—Peter Drucker

That flight from Los Angeles seems both recent and distant now. Sitting in the aircraft, observing the rivets and joints that kept us airborne, I couldn't have fully appreciated how that moment would reshape my understanding of strategy and leadership. The metaphor of seams, those critical points of connection that provide both structure and flexibility, has proven more powerful than I initially imagined.

As we conclude our exploration of the SEAM framework, it's worth reflecting on how far we've come while looking ahead to the challenges and opportunities that await. The future of strategy isn't about eliminating uncertainty or achieving perfect control—it's about building organizations that can thrive amid complexity and change.

Traditional strategic models emerged in an era when change was more predictable and organizational boundaries more defined. Today's environment demands something different. Through my experiences from commanding missile defense units to consulting with global corporations, I've witnessed firsthand how organizations struggle when they attempt to apply rigid frameworks to fluid situations.

The SEAM framework emerged from this reality. It represents not just a new approach to strategy but a fundamental rethinking of how organizations can maintain coherence while embracing change. The framework's success in diverse contexts, from military operations to corporate transformations and technological innovation, demonstrates its universal applicability.

FORCES SHAPING TOMORROW'S STRATEGIC LANDSCAPE

Several key forces will define the strategic environment of tomorrow:

The Acceleration of Change
The pace of technological advancement continues to increase, creating both opportunities and challenges. Organizations must develop the capability to assess and integrate new technologies while maintaining strategic focus. During my time leading military modernization efforts, we learned that success comes not from chasing every new technology

but from understanding which innovations truly enable strategic objectives.

The Rise of Complex Systems
The interconnected nature of modern systems means that actions in one area increasingly affect outcomes in others. My experience integrating regional air defense networks demonstrated how understanding and managing these connections become as important as the individual components themselves.

The Human Element
Despite advancing technology, human judgment and creativity remain crucial. Leading teams through complex transformations taught me that success depends not just on having the right systems but on building the right relationships and understanding.

BUILDING FUTURE-READY ORGANIZATIONS

The organizations that will thrive in tomorrow's environment share several key characteristics:

Adaptive Capacity
They develop what I call "strategic muscles," the ability to sense and respond to change while maintaining core

purpose. This isn't about being reactive but about building the capability to evolve purposefully.

Connected Intelligence

They create networks of insight, combining human expertise with technological capability. During our missile defense modernization efforts, we found that the most effective systems were those that enhanced rather than replaced human judgment.

Cultural Resilience

They build cultures that embrace change while maintaining stability. This paradox of being both firm and flexible defines successful organizations in complex environments.

THE FUTURE OF SEAM

The framework itself must continue to evolve, just as the organizations it serves must adapt to changing conditions. Through my work with diverse organizations, I've identified several areas for future development:

Integration with Emerging Technologies

Artificial intelligence, machine learning, and advanced analytics offer new possibilities for each component of the framework. The key lies in using these technologies to enhance rather than replace human strategic thinking.

Enhanced Assessment Capabilities
New tools for measuring and understanding complex systems will enable more sophisticated assessment approaches. However, we must remain focused on measuring what matters, not just what's easy to measure.

Expanded Application Domains
While the framework emerged from military experience, its principles apply across sectors. From health care to education, organizations facing complexity can benefit from SEAM's structured approach to adaptation.

LEADING IN AN AGE OF UNCERTAINTY

Future leaders must develop new capabilities to effectively implement the SEAM framework:

Strategic Perception
The ability to see patterns in complexity and identify opportunities in uncertainty becomes increasingly crucial. This isn't just about analysis but about developing intuition informed by experience and data.

Adaptive Decision-Making

Leaders must balance the need for decisive action with the flexibility to adjust as conditions change. My experience in military operations taught me that this balance is achievable through proper framing and continuous assessment.

Relationship Building

The ability to build and maintain relationships across organizational boundaries becomes even more important as systems become more interconnected.

THE PATH FORWARD

As we look to the future, several imperatives emerge for organizations seeking to implement the SEAM framework:

Embrace Complexity

Rather than trying to simplify complex situations, learn to navigate them effectively. The framework provides structure without imposing rigidity, allowing organizations to maintain coherence amid uncertainty.

Build Learning Systems

Create mechanisms for continuous learning and adaptation. This isn't just about gathering data but about building the capability to turn insight into action.

Maintain Strategic Focus

While embracing adaptability, maintain clear connection to core purpose. The framework's partial framing approach helps organizations stay focused while remaining flexible.

A FINAL REFLECTION

As my flight landed in Washington that day, I had no idea how far the concept of seams would take us. The framework that emerged has proven valuable across contexts I couldn't have imagined. Yet its core insight remains simple: The connections between things, whether physical components, organizational units, or strategic elements, are not weaknesses to be eliminated but strengths to be leveraged.

The future will bring challenges we cannot predict and opportunities we cannot yet imagine. Success will come not to those who attempt to control these forces but to those who learn to work with them effectively. The SEAM framework provides a way forward, offering structure without rigidity, direction without constraint.

As you apply these principles in your own context, remember that perfection isn't the goal. The strength of your strategy lies not in its flawlessness but in its ability to adapt while maintaining purpose. The seams in your organization, those points of connection and potential friction, are not flaws to be eliminated but opportunities to be embraced.

The future belongs to those who understand this truth: In a world of increasing complexity and continuous change, the ability to navigate uncertainty while maintaining coherence becomes the ultimate strategic advantage. Through the SEAM framework, organizations can develop this capability, turning the challenges of tomorrow into opportunities for growth and success.

May your journey be guided by this understanding, and may you find strength in the seams that connect your strategy to success.

ABOUT THE AUTHOR

Mike "Woody" Woodhouse is a seasoned leader forged by twenty years in Space and Missile Defense, where he mastered strategy in combat and collaboration with global allies. Raised in Corning, New York, he holds a marketing degree from Niagara University and dual master's degrees in leadership (UTEP) and military arts and science (Army Command and General Staff College).

As a certified defense strategist and lieutenant colonel, he commanded with distinction, culminating his career at the Space Development Agency by revolutionizing warfighter readiness with cutting-edge space technology.

Now in Northern Alabama, Woody's influence thrives. In 2020, he launched the Patriot Bros. Association (thepatriotbros.com), a nonprofit uniting the Air Defense Artillery community through scholarships, bold merchandise, and events like the Duck Shoot golf tournament.

ABOUT THE AUTHOR

As founder of Casa Di Legno Design LLC, he channels his creative edge into standout design solutions. Living with his wife, Stacey, and sons Maddox and Owen, he blends grit with heart.

In *SEAM: The Adaptive Strategy Framework for Leaders,* Woody shares a battle-tested framework from decades in the field, office, and home. With a laugh and a nod, he shows how embracing imperfection—those critical seams—helps leaders master today's chaos.